play like

Audio Ac...

PLA...

Speed • Pit...

Freddie King

The Ultimate Guitar Lesson

by Dave Rubin

To access audio visit:
www.halleonard.com/mylibrary

Enter Code
7178-7287-4323-0458

Cover photo: Tom Hill / Wire Image

ISBN 978-1-4803-5569-9

HAL•LEONARD®
CORPORATION
7777 W. BLUEMOUND RD. P.O. BOX 13819 MILWAUKEE, WI 53213

Visit Hal Leonard Online at
www.halleonard.com

CONTENTS

INTRODUCTION

"He taught me when to make a stand, when not to show your hand, and most important of all, how to make love to a guitar." —**Eric Clapton on Freddie King**

Unique among the giants of electric blues—and he was a big bear of a man—Freddie (originally "Freddy") King stood out due to his triple-threat abilities as an expressive singer, creative songwriter, and virtuoso guitarist. The book you now hold in your hands will do nothing to prepare you for the first category, and little for the second. However, this definitive, in-depth look at all the elements and techniques of his guitar style will definitely send you on your way to accurately copping the licks and riffs from a choice selection of the Texas Cannonball's extensive catalog of blues standards. Included are many of his famous instrumentals at which he was unexcelled. King was a bonafide guitar-slinger and, as we travel together along his unique blues highway from Texas to Chicago to Cincinnati and back to Texas, we will make all the important stops for you to acquire the personal guitar chops to stand your ground in any jam session or cutting contest. Hop on board!

The book is organized into several chapters, each focusing on different aspects of Freddie's complete guitar picture. Here's a quick rundown of what to expect:

Gear Fit for a Blues King

For all practical purposes, King brandished just two main axes. But, oh baby, what gorgeous tone he squeezed out of them.

Songs

Five complete King classics drawn from the '60s and '70s will be analyzed in detail in a logical, easy-to-understand way, eliminating the mystery but not the mystique.

Essential Licks

Every cool lick that you always wanted to know, but were afraid to ask!

Signature Riffs

King was a blues riff machine with a seemingly endless supply of memorable phrases. Here, we will stop and peruse 11 of his best creations.

Integral Techniques

Embellish or transform your playing with these tough and tender guitar moves.

Stylistic DNA

Find out what makes King so special and different from even his esteemed namesakes and predecessors, B.B. and Albert.

Must Hear

The legendary recordings guaranteed to educate, inspire, and entertain—and which belong in every guitar player's possession.

Must See

The DVDs, live concerts, and YouTube vids guaranteed to educate, inspire, and amaze.

ABOUT THE AUDIO

To access the audio examples that accompany this book, simply go to **www.halleonard.com/mylibrary** and enter the code found on page 1. This will grant you instant access to every example. The examples that include audio are marked with an audio icon throughout the book.

GEAR FIT FOR A BLUES KING

Guitars

As opposed to B.B., who became identified with one iconic style of semi-hollow guitar after caressing a wide variety of "Lucilles," and Albert, who made one unique, aggressive-looking solidbody instrument his mistress, Freddie King displayed his love of the blues with two classic Gibson models. The first, and the one played on his earliest King/Federal singles, was a 1954 Les Paul Goldtop with cream-colored P-90 "pups" and a wraparound combination bridge/stop tailpiece, similar to what Muddy Waters was playing in Chicago at the time. After signing with the Cincinnati-based label in 1960, Freddie released a string of 45 RPM singles that would become future classics, starting in the summer with "Have You Ever Loved a Woman" b/w "Hide Away." Up through "Heads Up" in the spring of 1961, the recordings clearly sound like the fat bite of the P-90s.

However, starting in mid-summer 1961, the unmistakable out-of-phase Varitone setting of a cherry red 1960–61 ES-345TDC is clearly audible on "Christmas Tears" and "Let Me Be." A new era in the sumptuous tone of Freddie King had begun with the thinline semi-hollow guitars. Along with the Varitone, the PAF humbuckers provided King with a wider selection of tones from which to choose, especially for the "surf" instrumentals that he would cut in waves until the mid-'60s. The cover of *Getting Ready* (1971) shows him playing a lesser 1965 model ES-345 with a sustain-sucking trapeze tailpiece.

By the late '60s, Freddie, like B.B., had upgraded to the deluxe ES-355 with ebony fingerboard, multiple binding on the neck and body, block inlays, and gold-plated hardware. A cherry 1967 model, purportedly once belonging to him, sold a few years ago and featured a stop tailpiece, thereby rendering inoperable the Vibrola whammy bar that he never used. The neck pickup was reversed, with the pole pieces facing the bridge pickup. Photos also reveal him with a walnut-finished ES-355. The fancy, richly appointed model would be his instrument of choice for the rest of his too short life.

Amps

Nailing down the amps used by members of Freddie King's generation is almost always a matter of speculation, as they often played whatever was provided for them in the studio and even on the road. Suffice it to say, they were usually '50s or '60s tube amps that came to be prized for their rich, fat distortion and sustain. Models which have been suggested as ones King "abused" include a 50-watt tweed Fender Twin (pre-1959), '50s Ampeg Gemini, Gibson GA-40, early-'60s Fender 4x10 Concert, Fender Dual Showman, and blackface Fender Super Reverb. The only one positively identified is the Fender Quad Reverb (1972–79) seen in the many videos from the era and likewise favored by Albert Collins later in his career. Essentially a 100-watt silverface Twin Reverb in a 4x12 cabinet and similar to the Super Six with 6x10 speakers, King seems to have "dimed" the volume and treble, with the bass, midrange, and reverb rolled off for an overwhelming, searing sound.

Picks

Contributing to the sharp, defined tone throughout his career was his use of a metal index fingerpick, as well as a plastic thumbpick that was suggested by Jimmy Rogers when King ventured to Chicago in the '50s.

Effects

C'mon, get real! This is original, real deal, postwar electric blues straight into the amp, man.

SONGS

I'm Tore Down
From *Freddie King Sings,* 1961

Within six months after signing with Federal Records, King had released 10 singles, with "I'm Tore Down" shuffling hard to #5 on the R&B charts. It has since become a fan and guitar player's favorite, resulting in popular covers by Magic Sam and Eric Clapton and is an excellent introduction to his vaunted style. Like virtually his entire extraordinary catalog of classics, it is an excellent tutorial in phrasing and note selection. For reference, the full transcription begins on page 8.

Intro

Though he obviously knew the fingerboard "Low Tide" to "High Rise," he regularly favored the "Albert King box," or the upper extension of the minor pentatonic scale, along with the root position of the composite blues scale as heard in the intro of "I'm Tore Down." The latter scale is a combination of select notes from the blues scale and the Mixolydian mode and was utilized to a degree by T-Bone Walker and substantially popularized by B.B. King.

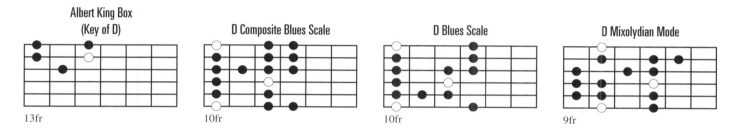

Albert King Box (Key of D) — 13fr   D Composite Blues Scale — 10fr   D Blues Scale — 10fr   D Mixolydian Mode — 9fr

Performance Tip: Execute the bends on string 1 with the ring finger, backed by the middle and index fingers, while using the index to pull *down* for the blues-approved quarter-step bend to the "true blue note" between the ♭3rd and major 3rd on string 3, in measure 4 (see photos).

Observe the way King "resolves" logically to the 5th (A) in measure 4, even though the bass and piano remain on the I (D7) chord. Like many blues guitarists of his generation and beyond, King was a "three-finger fretter." However, for the sake of efficiency, it is recommended that you use your pinky in measure 3, where it would handle the C note on string 2 (fret 13) while the ring finger would access the B (fret 12).

Chorus 1

Les Paul once said that he admired the playing of Eric Clapton because he always "told a story" with his licks and solos. In other words, they contained a beginning and an end, and maybe even a middle. Given his obvious and acknowledged influence on "Slowhand," it is thus no surprise to see King fill around his vocals with intelligent licks, each telling a little "vignette." He creates musical tension for the "beginning" either via bends (measures 7 and 11) or with a whiplash run up to the root on string 1 followed by a dynamic run down the scale (measures 15–16). The inclusion of the classic quarter-step pull to the "true blue note" in each lick adds "color commentary," anticipation for what comes next, and a salient detail.

Performance Tip: Check out how the octave root note always occurs on string 4—within logical reach of the ring finger in the root position of the minor pentatonic, blues, or composite blues scales. Likewise, as may be seen in measure 16, the ring finger should also be used for the 5th (A) on string 5. Of course, the "big story" is the way King chose the last note in each fill. The first sets the scenario with the ear-tweaking "true blue note," the second offers dramatic resolution via the root note of the I chord change, and the third concludes with the 5th (A), thereby advancing the "narrative" with anticipation to the next 12-bar chapter.

Verse 1 and Chorus 2

Stop-time, as featured prominently in the verses, produces taut, dramatic musical tension. The term refers to a short lick, riff, or chordal form followed by a measure or more of dynamic rest by the rhythm section. Below is a typical one-measure Chicago blues stop-time lick derived from the root position of the blues scale.

I'm Tore Down
Example 1

This next phrase is similar to a classic Freddie King stop-time lick and utilizes notes from the composite blues scale.

I'm Tore Down
Example 2

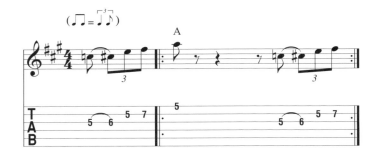

However, King opts to employ minimal means, using an implied D7 triple stop (beat 1 of measure 17) and an E♭7 double stop (beat 4). On the recording, a tenor sax plays a descending line (shown below) from the D Mixolydian mode in measure 20 as a way to connect from the I (D) chord to the IV (G) chord. These types of bass lines function as hip rhythm or lead guitar embellishments whether or not they are played in unison with the bass guitar.

I'm Tore Down
Example 3

Guitar Solo

King kicks the energy level of his swinging composition up a notch in a too brief 12-bar solo. Nonetheless, in an edifying display of his creativity, it seems longer, more expansive, and soaring, even with reliance on just the root and extension positions of the D composite blues scale.

Performance Tip: Despite the earlier admonishment to always attempt to utilize all four fret-hand fingers for efficient fretting, be aware that the use of the index and ring fingers is the best choice beginning in measure 46. Use the index finger to play the A note at fret 10 on string 2 (beat 4 of measure 45) and the D note at fret 10 on string 1 (beat 1 of measure 46). Now shift to the ring finger for the D note at fret 15 on string 2 in order to arrive at the most advantageous hand position in the extension position for the next eight measures. The index will handle the F note at fret 13 on string 1 and the ring finger will handle the G note at fret 15. When necessary, employ the middle finger for the A note at fret 14 on string 3. Back up the ring finger with the middle and index fingers for the numerous one-step bends. The three-note chromatic run in measures 50–52 may be easily accessed with the index, middle, and ring sequentially.

Here is a classic multi-bend, tension-inducing, Albert King-style lick that was also favored by Stevie Ray Vaughan. It's another reason to make the position and fingering your own.

I'm Tore Down
Example 4

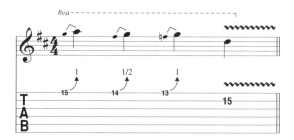

Performance Tip: Utilize the ring, middle, and index fingers in sequence to perform each bend. The one-step F-to-G "choke" on beat 3 will take some serious index-finger strength to execute, depending on string gauge. In measure 52, the A note at fret 17 on string 1 should be accessed with the pinky in order to maintain hand position. Hit the F note at fret 13 with the index finger (see photo).

I'm Tore Down
Full Song

I'M TORE DOWN

Words and Music by Sonny Thompson

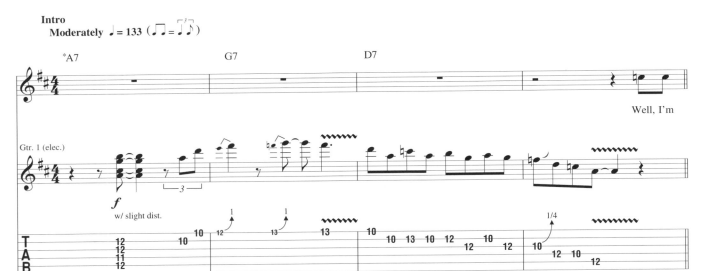

*Chord symbols reflect overall harmony.

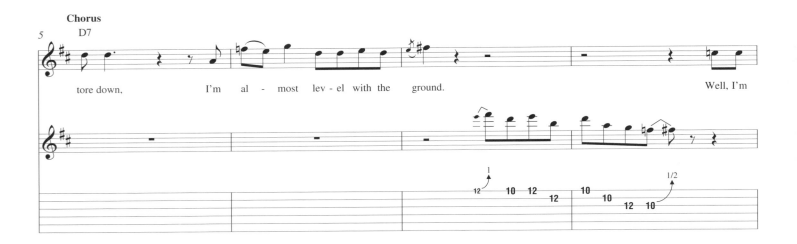

love you ba-by with all my heart and soul, ___ a love a-like mine _ a-will _ nev-er grow old. I
love you ba-by with all my mights. _ A love like mine _ is ___ out-ta sight. I'll

sim. on repeat   P.M.   P.M. - - -

love you in the morn-ing and in the eve - nin', too, ___ but ev-'ry time you leave me I get mad with you.
lie for you _ if you want _ me to, ___ I real-ly don't be-lieve _ your _ love is true. Well, I'm

Chorus

tore down, I'm al-most lev-el with the ground. Why'd

P.M. - - -   P.M. - -

To Coda ⊕

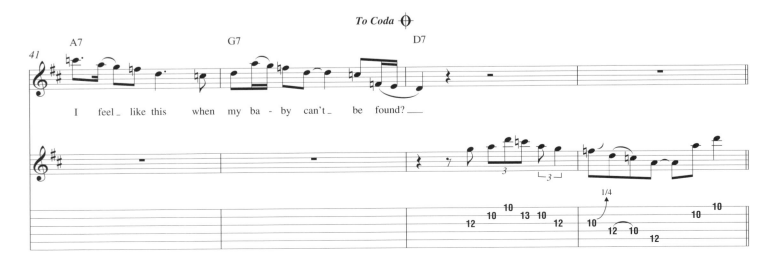

I feel _ like this when my ba-by can't _ be found? ___

Guitar Solo

The Stumble
From *Let's Hide Away and Dance Away with Freddy King*, 1961

Perhaps second only to "Hide Away" as the Freddie King instrumental of choice, "The Stumble" has been covered many times by artists such as Jeff Beck with the Yardbirds (1965), Peter Green in the Bluesbreakers (1967), Dave Edmunds in Love Sculpture (1968), and the late Bugs Henderson (1998). Compared to the iconic "Hide Away," "The Stumble" is a virtuosic recording, with only "Remington Ride" hot on its tail in the chops-required department. That said, "The Stumble" is a marvelous compendium of "Freddie-isms" and well worth the effort to learn precisely. As with all the songs in this book, I will hold your hand every note of the way. For reference, the full transcription begins on page 18.

Section A

The various sections in instrumental tunes are often referred to by section letters rather than "verse, chorus, bridge," etc. "The Stumble" has six letters, labeled A–F, with each 16 measures long. The chord progression is unusual for the blues, particularly the way it starts on the IV (A) chord, and critical to the scales, notes, and techniques King chooses as he builds his brilliantly crafted composition. Paramount to his approach is his exceptional combination of major and minor pentatonic scales. Except for measures 13–16, he relies on the root-position fingering of the C♯ minor pentatonic scale relative to the E major pentatonic scale, and the root octave position of the E minor pentatonic, respectively.

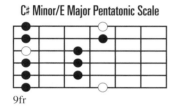

C♯ Minor/E Major Pentatonic Scale

9fr

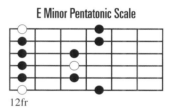

E Minor Pentatonic Scale

12fr

The pickup measure, measure 1, and measures 4–5 contain one of the signature major pentatonic motifs of the tune. And measures 13–14 open the door to an important blues guitar topic that could be an entire lesson in itself. Propulsive, descending 6ths derived from the E Mixolydian mode, similar to those in "Hide Away," drive the progression forward to the turnaround in measures 15–16 with inexorable energy. Here is the full E Mixolydian mode played in 6ths:

The Stumble
Example 1

Observe how King plays the 6ths line in "The Stumble" by avoiding the ♭7th degree (D) at fret 10 and the 4th (A) at fret 5 on his way down the scale. His decision may have been a combination of ease of execution, as the vertical fingering after the octave at fret 12, with its recommended middle (string 3) and ring (string 1) fingers, remains the same all the way down (see photo), or it may have been for expressive purposes, as skipping two of the scale degrees has the effect of increasing the perceived speed of descent.

Measures 13–16 are a significant part of the unique chord progression. Here are the basic "power chords" used for accompaniment (Gtr. 2), barely audible on the original recording:

The Stumble
Example 2

However, when playing rhythm, the following example shows an excellent way to expand upward to rich triads voiced in a logical manner without stepping on the guitar melody or bass.

The Stumble
Example 3

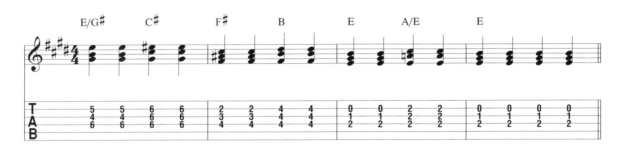

Section B

With a subtle exception, Section B is a reprise of Section A, the ostensible "head" of the tune. In measure 9 (I) of Section A, King comes into the stop-time bending the A (4th) at fret 14 on string 3 to B (5th) and he continues producing musical tension with repeated bending to the B through measure 12. In measure 25 (I) of Section B, however, he bends the D (♭7th) at fret 15 on string 2 to the root (E) before advancing to a similar approach as in Section A, based around bending A to B (measures 26–27). The effect is one of lifting the mood of the tune and building increased anticipation to the stop-time due to the higher pitch, despite the fact that it is the root note that generally tends to halt forward motion.

Performance Tip: Though King undoubtedly bent the D note in measure 25 with his ring finger, the pinky (backed by the ring, middle, and index fingers) would be most efficient, as it sets up the index finger for the B note at fret 12 in measure 26 (see photo).

Section C

"Dynamics" could have been his figurative middle name, as King slows the momentum and delivers 16 measures of exceptionally tasty improvisation while navigating the changes masterfully.

In measure 34, play the G on string 2 at fret 8 with the index finger and let it ring while accessing the D note at fret 10 on string 1 with the ring finger and the critical C#, the major-tonality-defining major 3rd of A, at fret 9 with the middle finger (see photos).

A quick move to place the middle finger on the G note at fret 8 on string 2 will be necessary in order to complete the measure efficiently with the index on the B note on string 1 at fret 7, followed by a repeat of the G and then the E note on beat 1 of measure 35 with the ring finger. Check out how measures 34–36 contain King's take on a classic blues move within a most useful minor pentatonic box for the blues (see diagram below). And here is the basic lick that Freddie's is derived from:

The Stumble
Example 4

E Minor Pentatonic Scale

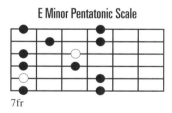

7fr

Performance Tip: In measure 37–38 (IV chord), King locks into one of the handiest blues guitar fingerings when he barres fret 5 with his index finger and rolls up the A composite blues scale to nail the harmony. Be sure to slide with your middle finger from B to C# on string 3 across the bar line. In measures 39–40 (V chord), hammer from the open fifth string with your index and middle fingers to arrive logically and smoothly at the root (B) target note at fret 2. Form the D/B (b7th/5th) dyad in measures 41–44 (I chord), which implies a bluesy, dominant tonality, with the ring and index fingers, low to high (see photo). Be sure to apply sufficient pressure with the ring and index fingers to produce a strong, clean sound when sliding into each downbeat.

Performance Tip: Measure 45 (I and VI chords) shows King recycling the D/B dyad with the ring finger sliding up to fret 12 on string 2, followed by the index striking the D note on string 1 at fret 10. You should then switch to the middle and index, low to high, for the A and C♯ notes, respectively. Maintain the fingering two frets lower for the too-cool blues bend demonstrated earlier. The figure below contains the Mixolydian dyad scale in 3rds and in the key of E from which measures 41–45 are drawn.

The Stumble
Example 5

Section D

Having established his well-oiled groove and cruising effortlessly as fluid lines, bends, and supercharged repeating patterns flow from his seemingly boundless reserve of improvisational fuel, King again builds to the finish in measure 48. Perhaps intuitively composing as he goes along, he connects Sections C and D across the bar line with the dominant D/B dyad after not pausing for a turnaround in order to perpetuate forward motion.

However, he is in no hurry, possessing total confidence in his abilities to control the speed of the journey, as may be seen in measures 50–52. Utilizing the aforementioned E minor blues box, with the addition of the 6th (C♯) on string 1 at fret 9, he manages to acknowledge the IV (A) and I (E) chord changes with relaxed, sinewy, twangy licks that lead seamlessly to measures 53–54 (IV chord) and the root position of the A composite blues scale.

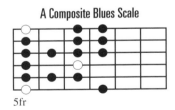

A Composite Blues Scale

5fr

Performance Tip: Deceptively simple in concept but exceptionally effective in practice, in measure 53, King glisses from B (2nd) to C♯ (3rd) on string 3 with his middle finger, followed by his index vibratoing and sustaining E at fret 5 on string 2. He then alters his phrasing to the classic hammer-on from C (♭3rd) to C♯, resolving to E in anticipation of measure 54, where he builds increased musical tension by repeating the A major-tonality-defining triplet three times. Barre strings 3–2 at fret 5 with your index finger, picking string 3 and hammering to fret 6 with the middle finger.

King recycles the rolling bass-string triplets from Section C for measures 55–56, resulting in a dynamic drop in register from the previous measures. In addition, he appropriates the basic approach of measures 9–12 of Section A (and measures 25–28 of Section B) for measures 57–64, where the extended usage of the bends from the root octave position of the E minor pentatonic scale serves to further pump up the forward motion to the turnaround in measures 63–64 and Section E.

Performance Tip: Measure 57 (I chord) stands out dramatically due to the relatively large interval leap unusual in the blues. Play the octave E at fret 12 with the index finger and the lower octave at fret 14 with the ring finger (see photo). Move quickly to string 3 for the bend to the "true blue note" in between the ♭3rd (G) and major 3rd (G♯), executed by pulling *down* with the index finger.

Performance Tip: King applies a different turnaround in measures 63–64 than in the previous Sections. Completely moveable to other keys, it involves barring strings 3–2 with the index finger at fret 12 in the root octave position of the E composite blues scale (see photo).

Following the root (E) note at fret 14 on string 4 with the ring finger, strike strings 3–2 while holding the barre and immediately hammer onto the G♯ at fret 13 with the middle finger to confirm the E major tonality, followed again by the root and then strings 3–2 at fret 14, barred with the ring finger to imply the change to the IV chord with C♯/A (3rd/root). In measure 64, repeat the barre, hammer onto the G♯, and run down the scale to the 5th (B) to imply resolution to the V (B) chord (even though the rhythm section remains on the I chord). The melodic, signature pickup into Section E (as seen in Sections A and B) ends the measure.

Sections E and F

King essentially reprises Sections A and B, with Sections E and F likewise functioning as the "head" of the composition, bookending the more improvisational middle Sections. Nonetheless, pay close attention to measures 73–76 and 89–92 in Sections E and F, respectively. In the former, King rakes down the root octave position of the E minor pentatonic scale over the stop-time IV (A) and ♭V (B♭[♭5]) changes. In the latter, he picks a descending and ascending run in the root octave position of the E minor pentatonic scale (with the crucial addition of the G♯ from the composite blues scale on the way up), which has the effect of "making time stand still," the famous description of Eric Clapton's King-inspired phrasing.

Performance Tip: In measures 75–76 of Section E, barre strings 3–1 with the index finger and upstrum with the pick, followed by the usage of the ring and index fingers through to the end of the run.

Performance Tip: Be aware that the B♭ (♭V) chord that appears in the 12th bar of each Section is actually an implied B♭°7 chord.

Diminished chords one half step above the IV chord in the blues compel the ear to want to hear resolution back to the I (E) chord next, as occurs in "The Stumble."

The Stumble
Full Song

THE STUMBLE

Music by Freddie King and Sonny Thompson

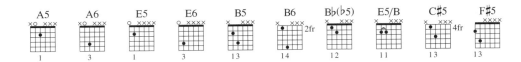

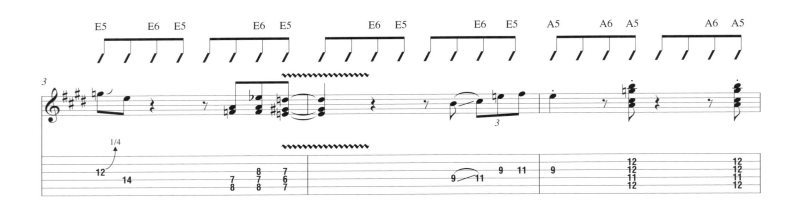

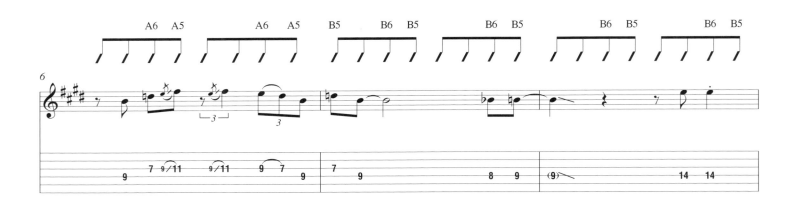

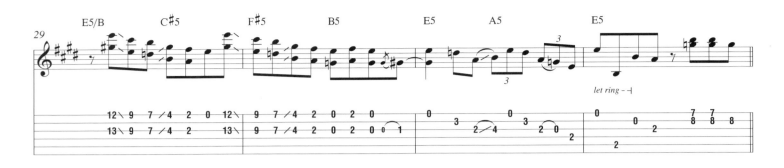

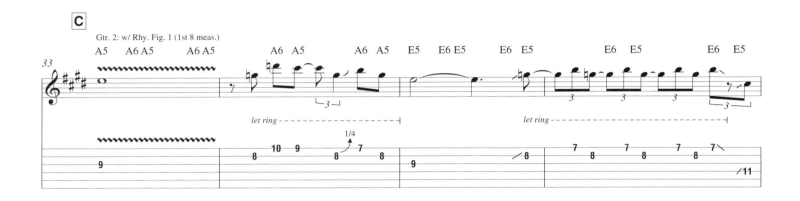

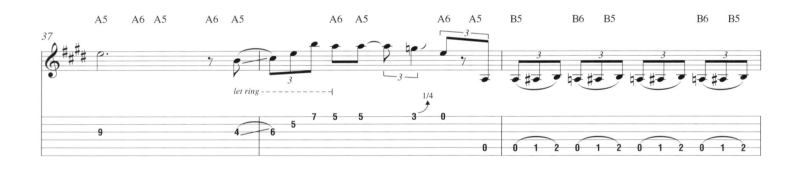

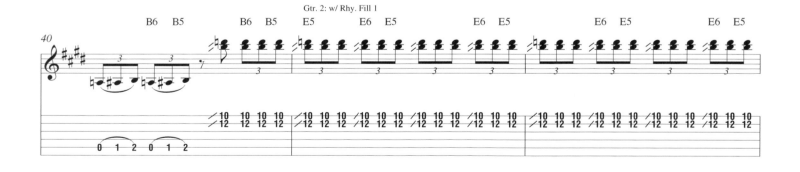

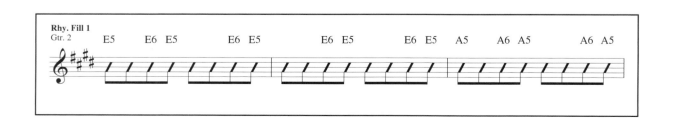

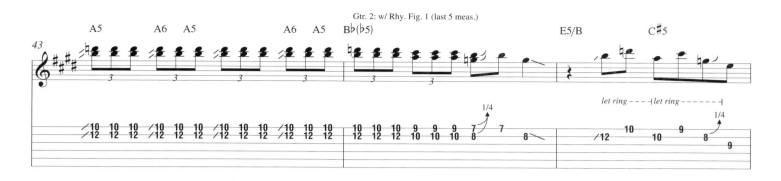

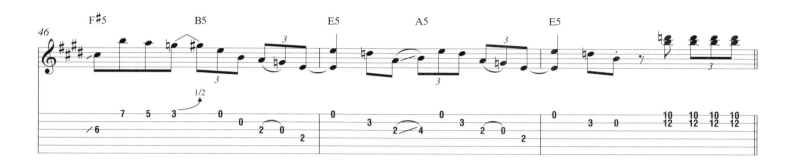

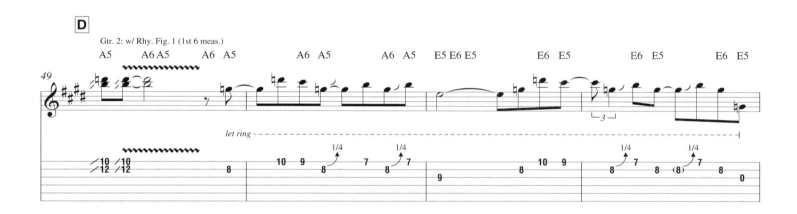

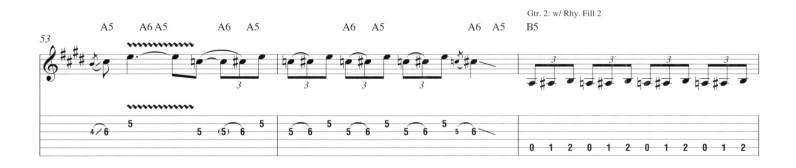

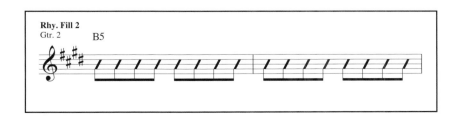

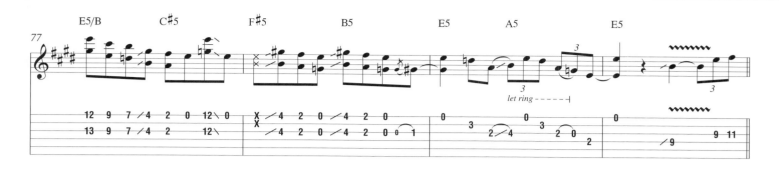

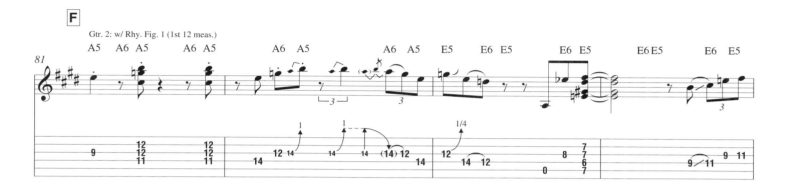

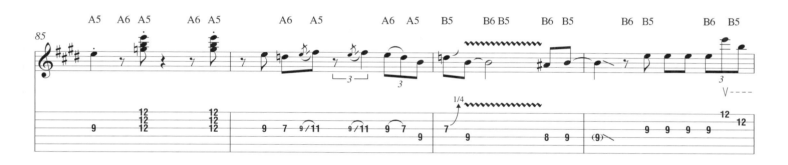

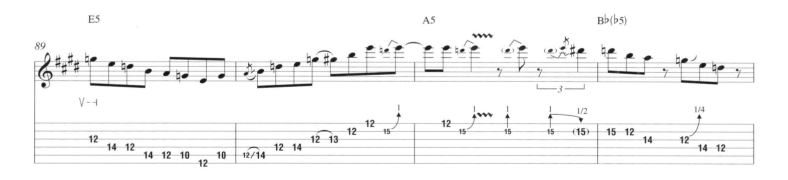

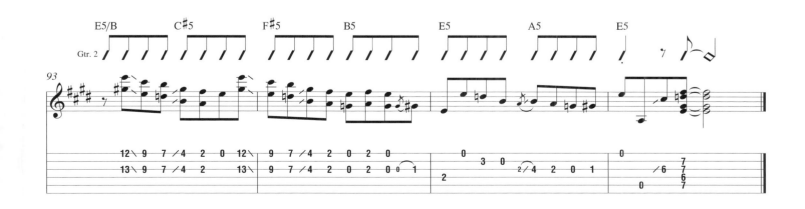

San-Ho-Zay
From *Let's Hide Away and Dance Away with Freddy King,* 1961

Another favorite Freddie King instrumental prized by blues and rock guitarists, "San-Ho-Zay" made it all the way to #4 and #47 on the R&B and pop charts, respectively. Well-known recording artists who have tried their hands at covering it include Junior Walker, Magic Sam, Albert King, and Luther Allison. For reference the full transcription begins on page 29.

Section A

There are multiple aspects to King's genius as a titan of electric blues guitar. One that powers "San-Ho-Zay," and is a lesson to take to heart by contemporary blues and rock guitarists, is the way he could create endlessly within the root position of the composite blues scale (Gtr. 1). Section A is the de facto "head" of the tune, exhibiting a primary and crucial characteristic of the blues whereby the G/E♭ dyad at fret 8 on strings 2 and 3, respectively, is repeated over all three chord changes as a signature motif producing gritty blues "harmony" and musical tension.

Performance Tip: As in classical or flamenco music, a full barre with the index finger across all six strings at fret 8 would theoretically be the most efficient method for accessing all the notes in the root position of the C minor pentatonic scale, along with the double stops. However, most steel-string guitarists would likely find it uncomfortable, even though it would, at the very least, make for a great exercise in building fret-hand strength. That said, barre strings 4–2 at fret 8 with the index finger, being careful to strike only strings 3–2 for the hip blues-approved G/E♭ (5th/♭3rd) dyad, which appears in every measure. Hence, you will be able to easily hit the B♭ (♭7th) note on string 4 at fret 8 held down by the index finger and the root (C) and 5th (G) at fret 10 on strings 4 and 5, respectively, with the ring finger. Know that you will need to shift your index finger to strings 6–5 at fret 8 for the F/C, which represents a second-inversion F chord with the 5th on the bottom.

The figure below contains a dyad scale in 4ths and 3rds that is related to the dyads in "San-Ho-Zay" and useful for blues and rock 'n' roll improvisation à la Chuck Berry.

San-Ho-Zay
Example 1

Performance Tip: Pull *downward* with the index finger for the "true blues," quarter-step bend of G/E♭.

Performance Tip: The cool "soul man" way to play the I (C), IV (F), and V (G) triads of rhythm guitarist Fred Jordan (Gtr. 2) would be to barre strings 3–1 with the index finger at the appropriate fret position and reach the notes on string 3 and 2 with the middle finger (see photos).

Section B

The progression expands to 16 measures via the addition of four more measures of the I (C) chord, resulting in eight measures instead of four. King takes advantage of the extra measures with the inclusion of dynamic stop-time in measures 19–20, which precedes the change to the IV (F) chord in measures 21–22. Where a lesser artist would next jump headlong into a solo, King opts to build incrementally with inventive thematic variations before arriving at the improvisational Sections D and E. In Section B, he essentially restricts his focus to strings 5–3 of the root position of the C minor pentatonic scale until he reaches the turnaround in measures 27–28. The result is classic blues guitar riffing. In measure 13, musical tension is produced on string 3 with a combination of the one-step bend from the 4th (F) to the 5th (G) and the quarter-step bend to the "true blue note" in between the ♭3rd (E♭) and major 3rd (E), resolving to the root (C) on string 4. Thereafter, similar variations occur through to measure 26.

Performance Tip: The example below is a good exercise for developing the technique necessary to execute the initial phrase fluidly so it may become a tasty ingredient in your "blues stew." Bend the F with the ring finger, backed by the middle and index. Bend the E♭ by pulling *downward* with the index. Play the C with the ring finger. Repeat the phrase as necessary!

San-Ho-Zay
Example 2

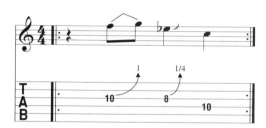

Among his many contributions to the language of electric blues guitar, King created a ransom of must-know turnarounds. Check out how the dyads in measure 27 imply movement from the I (C) chord (via G/E [5th/3rd in the key of C]) to the IV (F) chord (via A/F [3rd/root in the key of F]), even though the rhythm section stays on the I chord. Be aware that the G♭/E♭ dyad at frets 7 and 8, respectively, constitutes a "grace" dyad to add momentum to what follows and is emblematic of the unique organic nature of the blues. The following example contains the C Mixolydian mode harmonized in 3rds from which King derived his forms.

San-Ho-Zay
Example 3

Even "hipper" is the second-inversion Cm7 (5th in the bass) chord arpeggiated in measure 28. Below is the more typical five-note voicing with the octave 5th (string 2) and root (string 1) added on top.

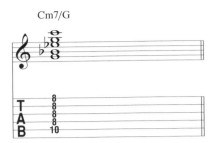

Cm7/G

Performance Tip: Use your ring finger on string 5 and barre strings 4–1 with your index finger (see photo).

Section C

In measures 29–36 (I chord) of Section C, King brilliantly expands on his original G/Eb dyad motif from Section A. As first shown in measure 29, he adds A/F at fret 10 to the harmony and proceeds to fashion a two-measure phrase by connecting it to the root position C minor pentatonic scale in measure 30 with emphasis on the pungent b3rd (Eb). Following a bass line pickup echoing the bass guitar on beats 3–4, King repeats the two-measure phrase almost verbatim, with the critical substitution of the b7th (Bb) in place of the b3rd as the target note. The result is a form of call and response within each two-measure phrase, as well as between the pairs of riffs. Call and response is a vocal tradition going back to the roots of the blues—the field hollers in the South, if not literally to Africa itself. As the blues and its offshoot, jazz, evolved over time, the dynamic practice of call and response became an integral part of both original American music genres.

Below are the locations of the prime target notes, in order of importance, as they appear in the root position of the C minor pentatonic scale.

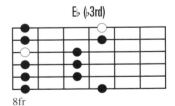

Eb (b3rd)

8fr

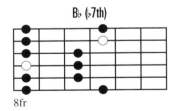

Bb (b7th)

8fr

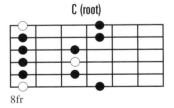

C (root)

8fr

There is no universal agreement as to what constitutes a target note, but close listening to the blues, and especially blues guitar, seems to bear out the b3rd (Eb), b7th (Bb), and root (C) notes. Understand the concept of a target note as a destination to be preceded by other notes in the scale. Both the b3rd and the b7th create desirable musical tension and anticipation to what may follow, including most prominently the root of the chord change. However, the root itself as a target note functions as resolution, halting forward motion and necessitating the start of a new musical idea or phrase. In the case of measure 12 of a 12-bar blues, or measure 8 of an 8-bar blues, where the root of the V chord is the target note, desirable resolution occurs in order to differentiate the start of another musical idea in the next 12- or eight-measure segment.

Section D

Finally feeling free to indulge his enormous improvisational gifts, King navigates the 12-bar chords with the grace of a Texas bull out for a midday stroll in the pasture. With his big feet firmly planted in the root position of the C composite blues scale, he acknowledges every change of harmony with subtle shifts of note selection.

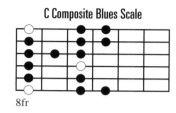

C Composite Blues Scale

However, take notice of the way he connects Sections C and D (measures 44–45) by anticipating the I (C) chord of the latter with major 3rd (E), 5th (G), and 6th (A) notes in the former resolving to the root (C) on beat 1. Again, one of the critical characteristics of the composite blues scale is the major 3rd, which confirms major harmony. The first example shows a most typical classic lick containing the major 3rd, while the second example contains the ♭3rd.

San-Ho-Zay
Example 4

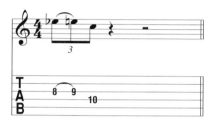

San-Ho-Zay
Example 5

Following his sly emphasis on the ♭3rd (E♭) target note in measure 45 for juicy tension, King alternates measures containing the prickly ♭3rd (45 and 47) with those featuring the harmonious major 3rd (46 and 48). Notice how he accesses the major 3rd in measure 48 by bending the ♭3rd at fret 11 on string 1 one half step from E♭ to E natural for a slinky effect, as opposed to the straight hammer-on from the ♭3rd.

Performance Tip: As confirmed in videos, King was a "three-finger" guitarist, utilizing his ring finger rather than his pinky, but it is recommended to employ the latter finger (backed by the ring, middle, and index) for the E♭-to-E bend.

Check out measures 49–50 (IV chord), where King, following the aforementioned protocol, avoids the major 3rd while highlighting the ♭3rd as a target note. Be aware how the ♭3rd of C becomes the ♭7th in the key of F, promoting forward motion back to the I chord. The example below offers a classic lick for the I chord containing both the major 3rd and the ♭7th.

San-Ho-Zay
Example 6

In measures 51–52 (I chord), he reverses the order of tension vs. release seen in measures 45–48 by featuring the major 3rd in the former and the ♭3rd in the latter. While King may not have thought about it deliberately, the effect creates tension and anticipation preceding the critical measure 9 juncture of a 12-bar blues (here, measure 53), where the V (G) chord appears for the first time in most progressions. Again, when we analyze his music, we see how King makes sure to acknowledge the V chord by bending up to the root (G) on string 3 from the ♭7th (F) in conjunction with the 4th (C), with both notes relative to the key of G instead of C. The smooth transition to the IV chord in measure 54 is facilitated by extending the two-note lick from measure 53 to beats 1–2 before the root (F) and ♭7th (E♭) make their welcome appearance.

Measures 55–56, the turnaround, are similar to Sections B and C.

Section E

Section E presents the climax of the improvisation. In measures 57–60 (I chord), King ratchets up the energy quotient by entering aggressively with propulsive, repeating riffs and a flurry of eighth notes. Once again, he creates tension by emphasizing the ♭3rd (E♭) in measure 57 while introducing a new sound in measure 58, where he works in the 2nd (D) in conjunction with the root (C) note. Then, in the blink of an eye, he strides up the C composite blues scale, hammering from the ♭3rd to the major 3rd (E) across the bar line of measures 58–59 on the way to string 1, where he peaks with the ear-tweaking, half-step bend of the 9th (D) at fret 10 to the ♭3rd. Observe how this is one of the rare occasions where you want to "Do the Freddie" and bend with the ring finger!

Also, check out the blues "box" in measure 59 in which King corrals his focus. It contains the 3rd, 5th, 6th, root, and 9th (the 2nd an octave higher) notes, which could be seen as from the C major pentatonic scale, in addition to the composite blues scale.

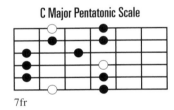

C Major Pentatonic Scale

7fr

Be that as it may, the harmonic results are conclusively major. Measure 60 provides dynamic contrast with repeated bends from the 4th (F) to the 5th (G) on string 3, producing subtle tension and anticipation leading smoothly to measure 61 (IV chord), where King wisely allows the E♭ to function as the ♭7th.

At this point, King appears to be anticipating the next chord change by a measure with his note selection, in a manner seen in the music of his namesake, B.B. King. The concept is clearly apparent in measure 62 (IV chord), where he executes the classic ♭7th (B♭) to root (C) bend on string 2 relative to the C chord change, followed by the root on string 1 and the bend repeated twice. King repeats the bend to the root in measure 63 (I chord) to maintain flow and momentum before he syncopates his phrasing around the 4th (F) bent to the 5th (G) in measure 64. It is a spectacular example of how he wrung every last drop of blues out of the root position blues scales.

Measure 65 (V chord) likewise gives the distinct impression of anticipating measure 66 (IV chord). Melodic analyzation in the key of F reveals the ♭7th (E♭), 6th (D), 5th (C), 4th (B♭), major 3rd (A), and root (F) notes. However, in measure 66, King once again exhibits his musical intelligence when he rakes down the root position of the C minor pentatonic scale in what *could* be seen as C minor harmony, when, in context, it contains the 5th (C), ♭7th (E♭), 9th (G), and octave 5th relative to F9!

The turnaround (measures 67–68) is essentially the same as Sections B, C, and D, except for resolution to the I (C) chord.

Sections F and G

Sections F and G are a virtual reprise of Sections A and B, the head of the tune, but in reverse order.

SAN-HO-ZAY

Words and Music by Freddie King and Sonny Thompson

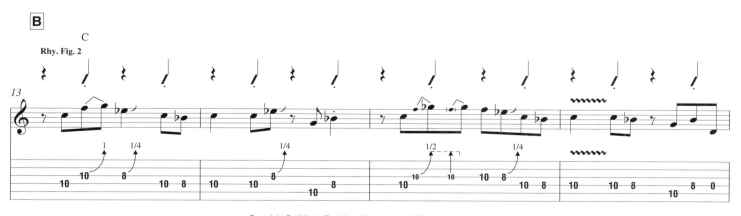

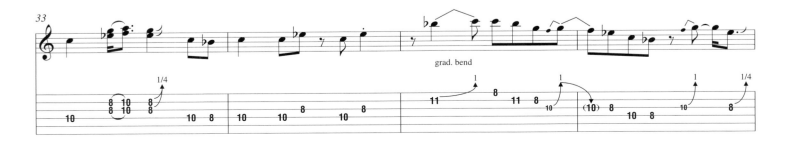

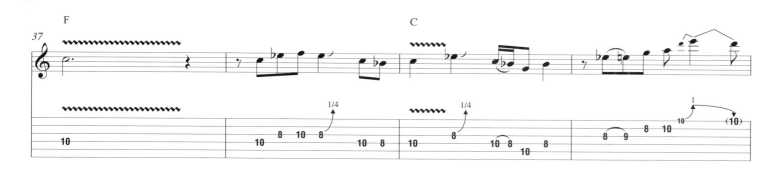

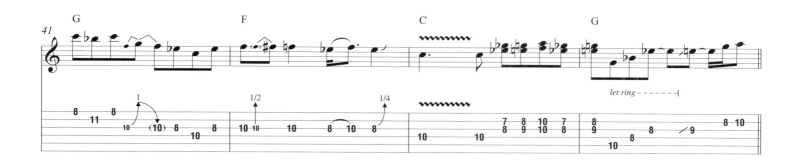

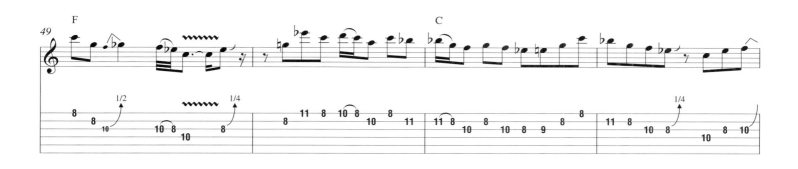

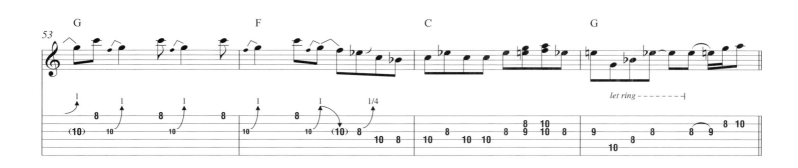

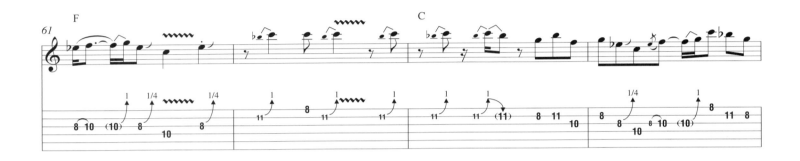

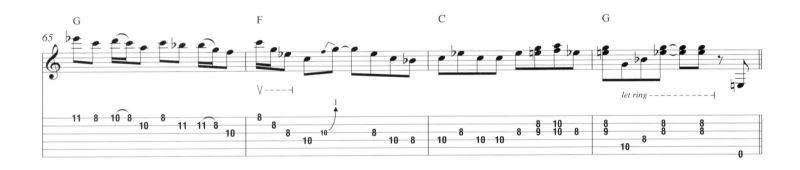

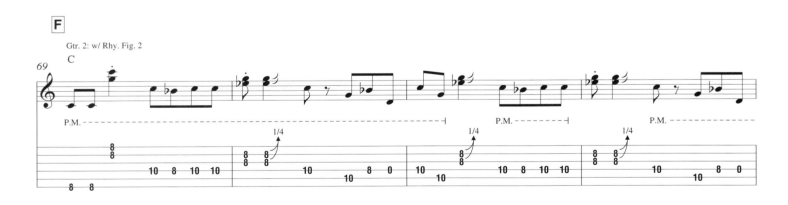

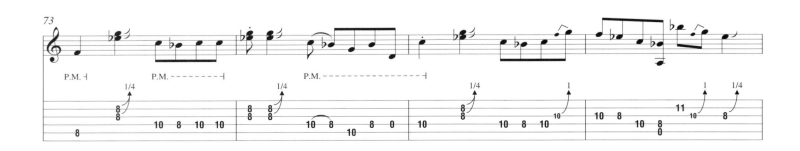

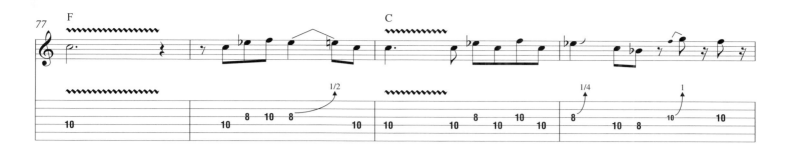

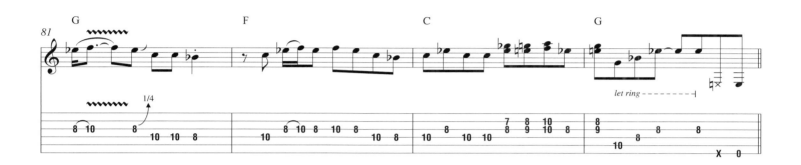

G

Begin fade   ***Fade out***

Gtr. 2: w/ Rhy. Fig. 1 (till fade)

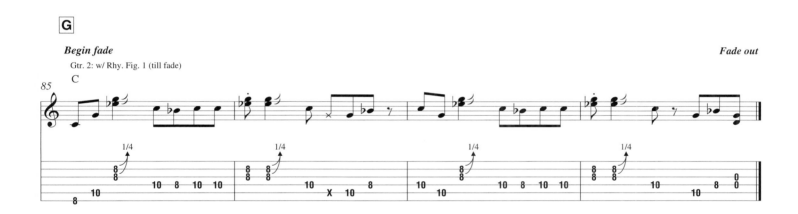

Remington Ride
From *Freddy King Gives You a Bonanza of Instrumentals*, 1965

Freddie King's most spectacular instrumental is a 5:44 epic in terms of length, breadth, and six stunning, improvised solos likely performed on his steely-sounding Gibson ES-345. Originally recorded by steel guitarist Herb Remington in the Western swing orchestra of Hank Penny in 1949, and in 1961 with studio cats at a blistering tempo (and first released by Freddie on the compilation *Rhythm & Blues Artists Sing Country Songs* in 1964), King interprets the slithery steel licks with uncanny finesse. The story goes that King/Federal Records head honcho Syd Nathan heard his star guitarist jamming on the tune in the studio and requested that he record it for the label. Apparently the two had been butting heads on finding "country" music appropriate to record, but finally agreed and produced a masterpiece. Suffice it to say, the "King" version, in both meanings of the word, swings more than the original.

"Remington Ride" is composed of two related 16-measure progressions: The first is referred to as "A" and contains E9 (six measures), B7 (two measures), A7 (two measures), C7 (two measures), E7–C♯7 (one measure), F♯7–B7 (one measure), and E (two measures). The second is referred to as "B" and contains A7 (four measures), E9 (four measures), F♯9 (four measures), and B7 (four measures). In the vernacular of jazz and music from the classic American songbook before most rock 'n' roll, the resulting combination, with the A section repeating after the B section, is referred to as "ABA form," as opposed to "verse, chorus, verse, etc.," and is 48 measures long. It should be noted that the original version was in the more typical AABA form, at a total of 64 measures. For reference, the full transcription begins on page 40.

Section A

Along with Section B, Section A functions as the A section of the head of the tune. As Gtr. 1, King smoothly streamlines Herb Remington's original steel-guitar melody in order to create an intelligently reasonable facsimile with just the root (E), 2nd (F♯), and 3rd (G♯) notes from the E major scale, along with the 5th (B) and 6th (C♯) in the pickup measure. However, he appears to be playing out of two positions. The pickup notes and measures 4 and 8–16 are plucked from the root position of the E major (or the relative C♯ minor) pentatonic position, while the melody in measures 1–3 and 5–7 is derived from a section of the seventh-position E major scale. The root notes are shown as white dots in the following diagrams. Both positions logically entail the familiar use of the index and ring fingers without changing fret location.

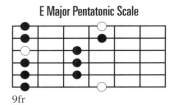

E Major Pentatonic Scale

9fr

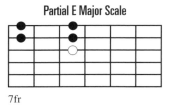

Partial E Major Scale

7fr

Performance Tip: All bends at fret 11 on string 3 are to be played with the ring finger, backed up by the middle and index.

Section B

Each of the four chords sport catchy melodic riffs drawn from the relative composite blues scale. Harmonically, they move in four-measure increments: IV (A7), I (E9), II (F♯9), and V (B7). The riffs build dramatically upward in pitch to the V chord, where the momentum is reversed in a descending line.

Measures 17–20 (IV chord) quite logically utilize the root (A), 3rd (C♯, bent up one step from B), and 5th (E) from the major scale, comprising an A major triad. (**Caveat:** The half-step bend to the ♭3rd (C), instead of C♯, in measure 18 is possibly a mistake, though not crucial, as it is the typical *blues* note.) The following figures show the relevant scale fragment and its related major triad, respectively. The soloing strategy of playing out of scale positions which relate directly to the fretboard location of the appropriate chord is more typical of steel guitar players than six-stringers but is an exceptionally useful one for the latter "twangers" to have.

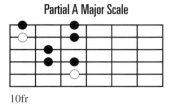

Partial A Major Scale

10fr

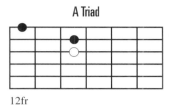

A Triad

12fr

Performance Tip: Bend up to the C♯ from the B at fret 12 with the ring finger, backed by the middle and index. Besides having increased strength, your hand will be in the perfect position to access the A note with the index finger. In measure 19, hit the E note by rolling the ring finger onto string 1 following the bend to the C♯.

Measures 21–24 (I chord) continue with the concept found in measures 17–20 while also employing two common tones, B and E, to facilitate the transition. Even simpler in approach, it basically utilizes just the 5th (B) and root (E) notes. However, adding to the melody while injecting a welcome shot of spicy "blues power" is the ♭5th (A♯ as notated, or B♭) at fret 11 as a "grace" note preceding the B at fret 12. See how the notes relate to the upper register of the root octave E blues scale and the E major triad.

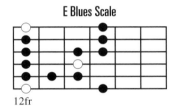

E Blues Scale

12fr

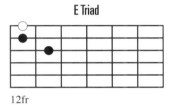

E Triad

12fr

Be aware how having the A♯ one half step above the A of measures 21–24 contributes to the sense of forward motion and uplift and that the way it most typically appears is on string 3 at fret 15 of the E blues scale.

Performance Tip: Play the A♯ with the index finger, the B with the middle finger, and roll the middle finger over to string 1 at fret 12 for the E note.

In measures 25–28 (II chord), King emphasizes the 5th (C♯) and ♭7th (E) notes, picked from the F♯ Mixolydian mode and an F♯7 voicing residing nearby.

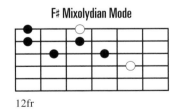

F♯ Mixolydian Mode

12fr

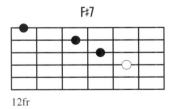

F♯7

12fr

Performance Tip: It would be best to play the B♯ with the middle finger and the C♯ with the ring finger on string 2, leading smartly to the E note on string 1 with the index finger.

King expands his color palette to include a broader swath of notes from the B composite blues scale for the V (B) chord in measures 29–32. In addition, he phrases his slippery line of descending tones exclusively on string 1 to further emulate the glissing characteristic of steel guitar.

Performance Tip: With the index finger, slide from F♯ (5th) to D♯ (3rd) and from E (4th) to C♯ (9th) in measure 29. With your index still at fret 9, play the D♯ at fret 11 with the ring finger, followed by the C♯ and D at frets 9 and 10, respectively, with the index and middle fingers. In this manner, you will end with the index finger on C♯, which will be sustained into measure 32, where the pickup back into the A section of the head in Section C reappears.

Section C

With little variation, Section C duplicates Section A and acts as the run-up to the spectacular improvisation of Sections D and E.

Section D

King swings like mad in his first 16-measure solo over section A in a magnificent display of his unexcelled powers in the root octave position of the E composite blues scale. In measures 49–54 (I chord), he puts on a string-bending show with his brawny ring finger. He utilizes it in measure 49 to stretch the 9th (F♯) one step to the sweet, major-tonality-defining 3rd (G♯), while in measure 50, he pushes the 4th (A) one step to the 5th (B) on string 3. The highlight of the show, however, occurs in measure 53, where he "piggybacks" three ascending, soaring string "chokes" to the ♭3rd (G), major 3rd, and 4th. The musical tension and anticipation created by this type of maneuver is unparalleled in blues guitar.

Performance Tip: As always, back up ring-finger bends with the middle and index fingers even as you advance up the fingerboard. Be cognizant of the control necessary to execute a series of various bends on one string. The following is a good exercise to help develop the skill using the ring finger.

Remington Ride
Example 1

Measures 57 and 59 (IV and ♭VI chords, respectively) feature the most subtle of all blues guitar bends with the index finger. Though more common as a quarter-step "bump" to the "true blue note" on string 3, the half-step bend as shown also produces a singularly expressive and fluid effect due to the release to the original pitch that follows. The exercise below is a classic lick with a half-step bend on string 2 and a quarter-step bend on string 3.

Remington Ride
Example 2

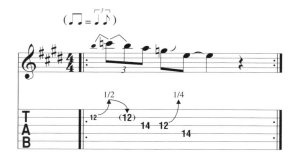

Section E

The second 16-measure solo contains breathtaking energy and dynamics as King flexes his superhero chops. The aggressive eighth-note unison bends in measures 65–66 (I chord) would be standard blues-rock fare except for the breakneck tempo.

Performance Tip: King undoubtedly used his ring finger, perhaps backed up by his middle finger, for the bends on string 2. But, as we are not postwar blues guitarists, or at least not self-taught post-WWII blues guitarists, we should utilize our pinky finger for the bends, backed, of course, by the ring and middle fingers. The wisdom of this approach should be even more evident in measures 68–70, where bending the D note at fret 15 on string 2 with the pinky and requisite backup fingers will logically place the index at fret 12 for the B note in measure 70. Just as important, your hand will now be perfectly located to access the A note on string 3 at fret 14 with the ring finger.

Performance Tip: In measure 71 (V chord), bend the G note on string 3 at fret 12 with the index finger by pulling *downward*. Even with lighter gauge strings, this requires a certain amount of strength. Below is an exercise to help develop the requisite index-finger chops.

Remington Ride
Example 3

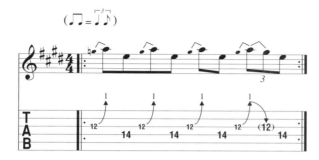

Section F

Section F is essentially a recap of Section B and makes for a dramatic, uplifting move via the chords moving up a 4th from the key of E (Section E) to the key of A (Section F).

Section G

Section G is similar to Section A.

Section H

King soars dynamically upward to begin his third 16-measure solo, virtually exploding with exuberant energy. Years before the late Who drummer Keith Moon offered his sage dictum that "People only remember your entrance and exit in a solo," King instinctively enters with a bang, bending the 4th (A) a penetrating one step to the 5th (B) at fret 17 on string 1 in the "Albert King box." As is his wont in the improvised sections of the tune, he favors riffing away on strings 2–1 in measures 113–118 to stay above the sonic space of the band. Contributing mightily to the newfound intensity in Section H are the unison bends (see photo) appearing in measures 116–117 and the stunning triplets in measures 121–122 (IV chord).

In the latter, King not only freely exhibits his athletic chops, but also his advanced concept of note selection with the inclusion of the ♭5th (B♭) blues note. Alternating the pull-off from the ♭5th to the 4th adds another dimension to the dynamic phrasing not in evidence when each triplet is identical.

Remington Ride
Example 4

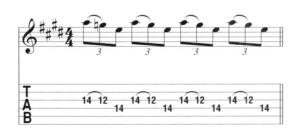

Performance Tip: Alternate the ring finger with the pinky at fret 14 and 15, respectively, on string 3.

This example contains a classic variation, with the triplets on strings 2–1.

Remington Ride
Example 5

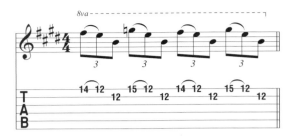

Performance Tip: Alternate the pinky and ring fingers on string 1 while barring strings 2–1 with the index at fret 12.

Section I

The fourth 16-measure solo has King again proffering propulsive triplets in dynamic counterpoint to long, languid bends. The former occurs in measure 133 (I chord), with the root (E), ♭7th (D), and 5th (B) notes derived from the octave "Albert King box" of the E minor pentatonic scale. You should know for future reference that the three notes strongly imply an E7 tonality to complement the chord change.

Performance Tip: In order, use your ring, index, and middle fingers.

Measures 136–137 (V and IV chords, respectively) feature a one-step bend at fret 15 (G) across the bar line, briefly giving the impression of time slowing down.

Performance Tip: King most certainly bends with his ring finger, necessitating a position change from the one-step bend of the ♭7th (A) to the root (B) at fret 17 on beat 1 of measure 136. Nonetheless, if the pinky, backed by the ring, middle, and index fingers, is utilized instead, it again allows the index to access the E on string 1 at fret 12, thereby returning the hand to the most advantageous location for the root octave position of the E minor pentatonic scale.

Section J

With some variation, Section J is a repeat of Section B.

Section K

Section A revisited.

Section L

In a continually amazing display of virtuosity, King discovers new ways to phrase within the same scale positions for maximum musical expression in his fifth 16-measure solo. In addition, with the end of his improvisation fast approaching in Section M, he reaches a climactic moment beginning in measure 184 (V chord) and continuing straight through measures 185–186 (IV chord) and concluding in measure 187 (♭VI chord). In a brash move creating thrilling musical tension in the extreme upper register of his ES-345, King whips back and forth between the D and B notes on string 1 at frets 22 and 19, respectively. He caps his guitar-slinging escapade by bending the D one step to the E before returning from the rarified air to the root octave position of the E minor pentatonic scale.

Performance Tip: In an exception to the "rule," the index and ring fingers can be used to play the B and D notes, given the closer fret locations on the upper fingerboard (see photo).

Section M

The sixth, and final, 16-measure solo does not disappoint, as King swings his hardest, phrasing with a rocking syncopation that drives the progression forward. Once again contributing to the surging forward momentum are snappy triplets, which appear in measures 196–197 (I chord). They constitute the third set played by King within his solos and contain the same notes as in measures 121–122 of Section H, but an octave higher. As with the triplets in measure 133 of Section I, they are plucked from the "Albert King box," but on strings 2–1 and with the addition of the ♭5th (B♭) from the blues scale.

Performance Tip: Alternate the ring finger with the pinky at frets 17 (A) and 18 (B♭), respectively, on string 1, while using the index finger at fret 15 (G). The ring finger is available after the index and is to be employed for the E on string 2 at fret 17.

Observe how King keeps the emphasis on string 1 in measures 193–200, letting his big, red, semi-hollow body "blues bird" soar and sing with a sweet 'n' sour tone that he obviously relishes. The result is an even greater degree of musical tension and a literal high point. In measures 200–208, he takes the register down a notch or two with a series of descending licks in the root octave position of the E minor pentatonic scale. Appearing prominently are bends and releases moving to the next lower note in the scale on strings 2–3, which add fluidity and a vocal-like element so crucial to authentic blues guitar. The exercise below involves strings 1–3 to strengthen your chops for the technique.

Remington Ride
Example 6

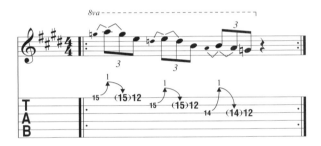

Section N

King returns dramatically to Section B one last time following his ultimate improvised solo in Section M. However, in measures 212, 216, and 220, he inserts a stinging fill from the root octave position of the E minor pentatonic scale as opposed to just sustaining the last note of the melody. Once again showing his intelligent, intuitive sense of composition, he makes the first fill (A chord) the longest and fastest, with the second one (E chord) less "note-y" and the third one (F♯ chord) consisting of only two notes. Pay attention to the way that he avoids playing the root note of each chord change last, thereby encouraging the listener to want to hear what comes next while also increasing forward momentum. Measures 221–224 (V chord) are similar to Section F.

Section O

Section A repeated.

Section P

King ends his bluesified "Opus de Western Swing" with an eight-measure coda consisting of the melody from measures 13–16 of Section A repeated twice and concluding with the I (E9) chord (measure 247). When joined with measures 237–240 of Section O, it makes for a total of three repeats. While less prevalent in the blues, this type of ending may be found in swing jazz and pre-rock pop music.

REMINGTON RIDE

Words and Music by Herb Remington and Hank Penny

Remington Ride
Full Song

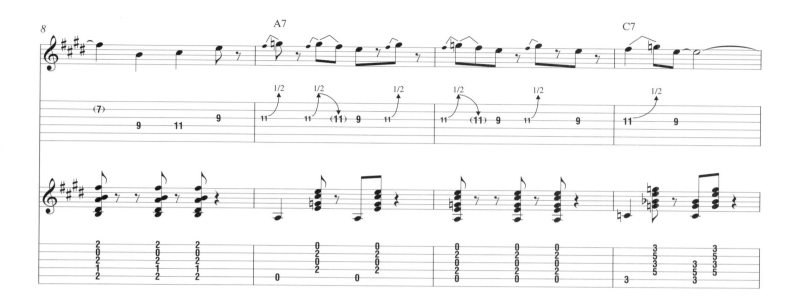

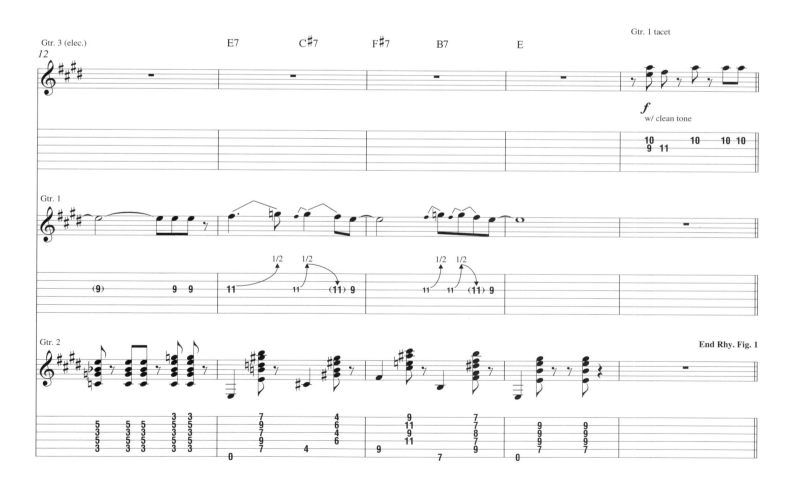

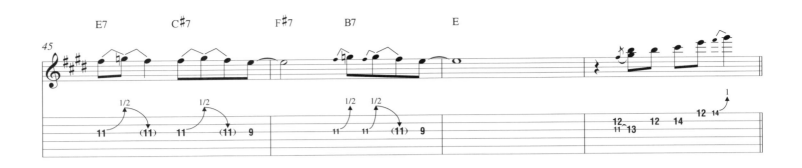

D

Gtr. 2: w/ Rhy. Fig. 1

*Played as even eighth notes.

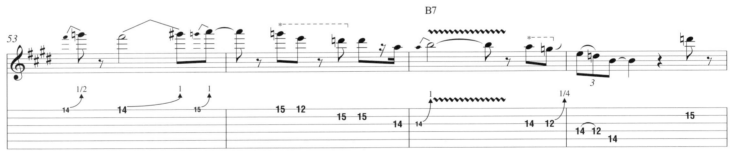

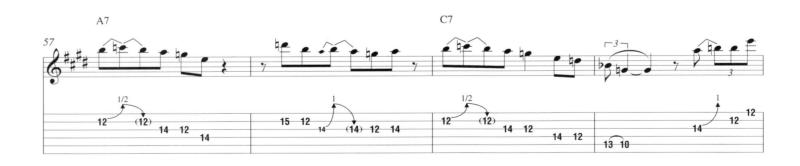

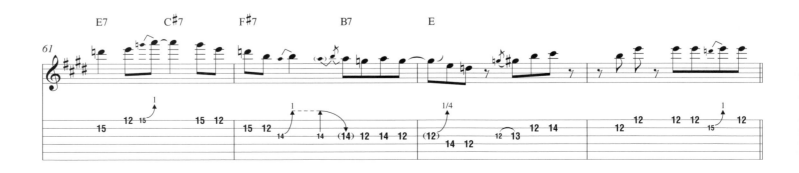

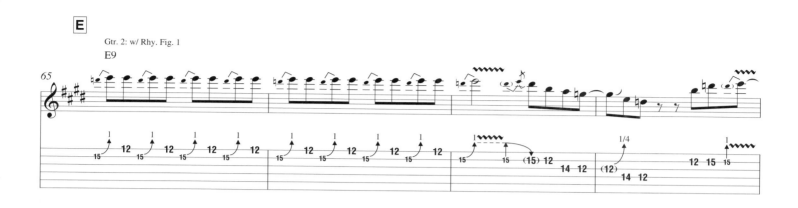

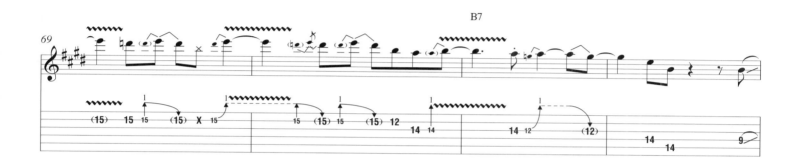

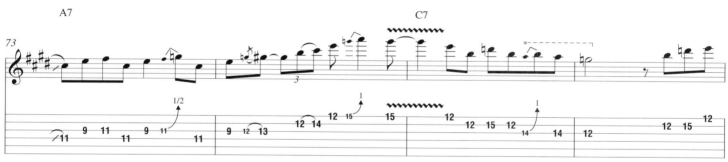

*Played behind the beat.

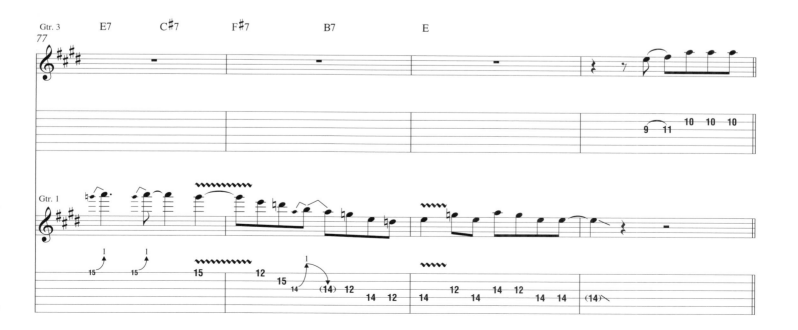

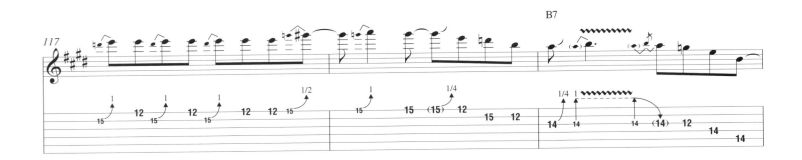

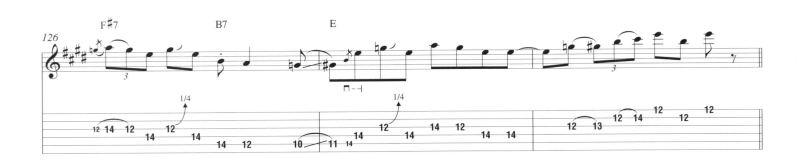

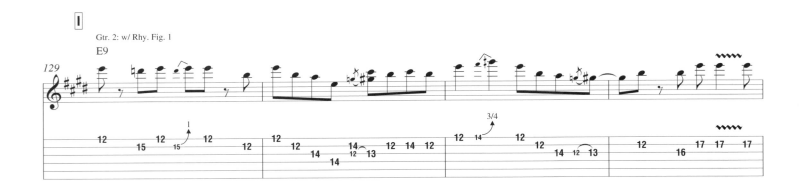

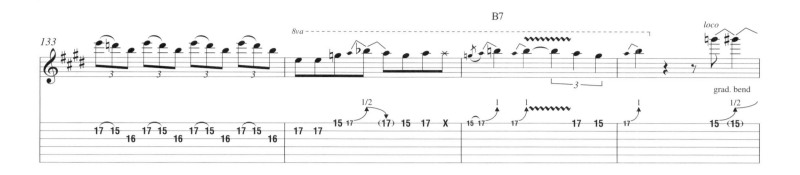

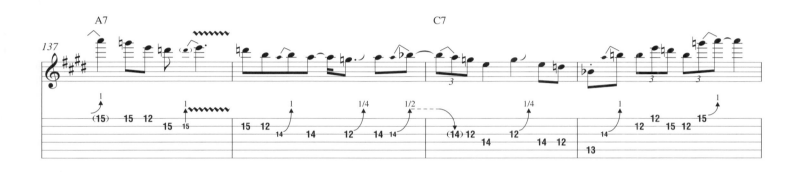

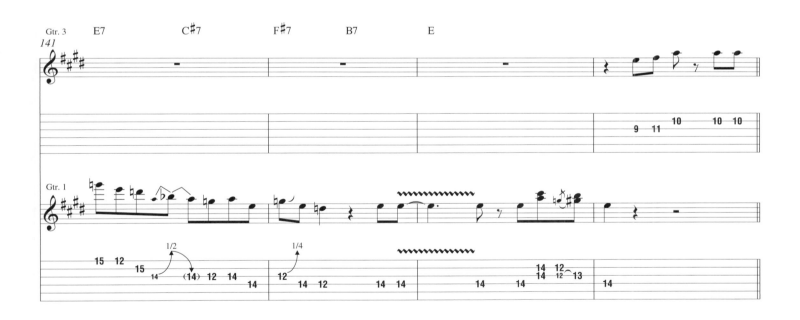

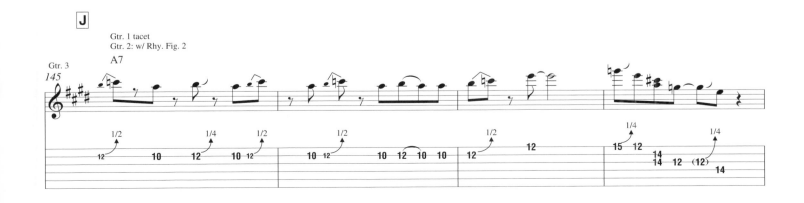

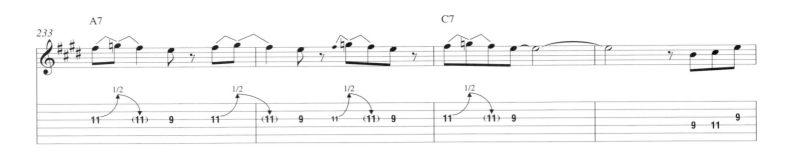

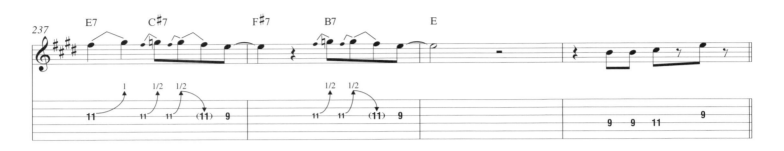

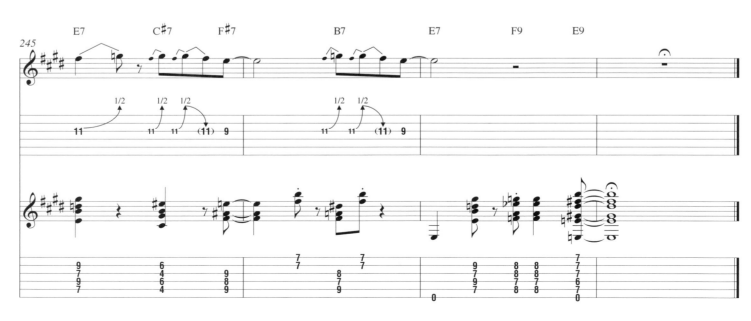

Going Down
From *Getting Ready...*, 1971

Written by Don Nix and originally recorded by Moloch on their eponymous debut in 1969, "Going Down" represents perhaps the hardest blues-rocking track ever cut by Freddie King. Jeff Beck also covered it with his Group in 1972 and it has been subsequently recorded by many other artists. The tune was re-released on *The Best of Freddie King: The Shelter Years* in 2000. The full transcription begins on page 57.

It consists of 12-measure verses and choruses played in 16th notes (Gtr. 2), but does not contain standard 12-bar blues chord changes. Instead, it is in an ABC arrangement with section A containing D5 (one measure), D5–C5–G5–F5 (one measure), and D5 (two measures) chords and section B containing G5 (one measure), D5–C5–G5–F5 (one measure), and D5 (two measures) changes. Section C contains A5 (one measure), D5–C5–G5–F5 (one measure), and D5 (two measures) changes.

Intro

The eight-measure intro utilizes measures 1–8 of the verse or chorus.

As Gtr. 1, King squeezes out juicy, arcing, sustained bends in the root position of the D minor pentatonic scale.

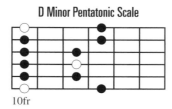

D Minor Pentatonic Scale

10fr

As will be seen, King uses the "modal" approach as his soloing strategy, whereby he mainly phrases around the D tonality as opposed to navigating each individual chord change. However, as will become apparent as we work through the song and transcription, he still, perhaps intuitively, emphasizes choice notes related to the changes. In measure 6, he twists the phrasing to his will in a descending line that actually mimics his vocal melody with the D, C, G, and F root notes two octaves above those played by Gtr. 2.

Chorus

In a classic call and response, King fills in between his vocal lines with mainly short, tart, bluesy phrases ending on either the root (D) or ♭7th (C) over the I (D) chord. The root, of course, halts forward momentum, while the ♭7th encourages it. The exception is in measure 13 (IV chord), where the D functions as the 5th and anticipates the I chord in measure 14.

The "Art of the Fill": Equally important instrumentally in the blues and blues-based music as solos, fills may offer dynamics between vocal lines, as well as contributing momentum. In a sense, fills are a microcosm of a blues solo inasmuch as they either create musical tension or resolution with generally the last note in the phrase. Quite simply, tension or anticipation may be created with the ♭7th (C), as shown in measures 9, 11, and 12, and resolution may be created with the root (D), as seen in measures 13 and 20.

Verse

As mentioned, the verses contain the same chord changes as the choruses. In addition, they feature the same approach regarding fills. Observe, however, how the critical tension-inducing ♭3rd (F) is utilized in measure 23 (I chord), while resolution is achieved with the root (D) in measures 21 and 31 (I chord) and with the root (G) in measure 25 for the IV (G) chord.

Performance Tip: Check out the location of the ♭3rd in all five "boxes" of the D minor pentatonic scale, which are moveable to all other keys. ♭3rds are represented as white dots in the diagrams below.

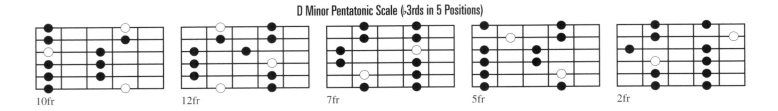

D Minor Pentatonic Scale (♭3rds in 5 Positions)

10fr   12fr   7fr   5fr   2fr

Guitar Solo

In a somewhat unusual move, even for the gifted Texas Cannonball, King produces a memorable 12-measure solo in the manner of older forms of pop music and jazz standards by interpreting the vocal melody with skill, creativity, and panache. But instead of reproducing the brisk, compact phrasing of "I'm going down," he tends to stretch his edited version of the melody to produce musical tension, as dramatized with bends in measures 33 and 37, as well as in measure 41 (V chord), where he either sings "back to Chattanooga" or "big feet in the window." In measures 34 and 38 (the D5–C5–G5–F5 changes), he descends through the octave extension position, or "Albert King box," of the D minor pentatonic scale in sync with the beats to imply the vocal line, though the pitch of the notes does not correspond to the vocals or the root note of the changes. However, in measure 39, he relocates to the root position, where he essentially plays the root notes, which precedes firm resolution to the root note (D) of the I chord in measures 43–44.

Outro-Guitar Solo

King rides out his heavy blues-rocking tune with searing, high-register bends in the octave D minor pentatonic "Albert King box" through measure 63 and the beginning of the fade. Similar to, if not even more intense than, the guitar solo, it also contains a classic Albert King technique across the bar line between measures 64–65. The C at fret 13 on string 2 is bent one step to D and then raised another half step to D♯ without being released or struck again. It is an exceptionally dramatic and tension-producing technique worth acquiring. The following is an effective exercise for its development.

Going Down
Example 1

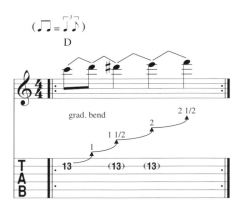

Performance Tip: Execute the bends in the transcription with the pinky backed up by the ring, middle, and index fingers, and, in the previous exercise, with the ring finger backed up by the middle and index.

GOING DOWN

Words and Music by Don Nix

Going Down
Full Song

Intro
Moderately slow ♩ = 84

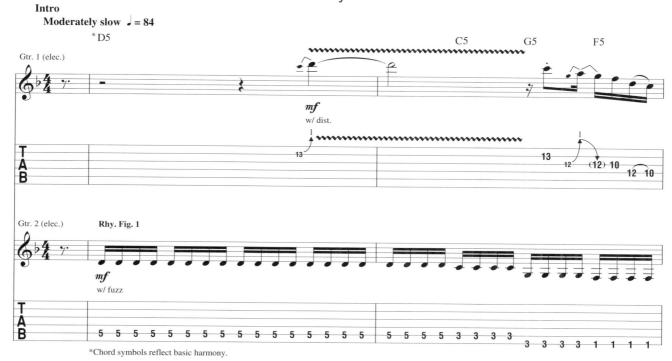

*Chord symbols reflect basic harmony.

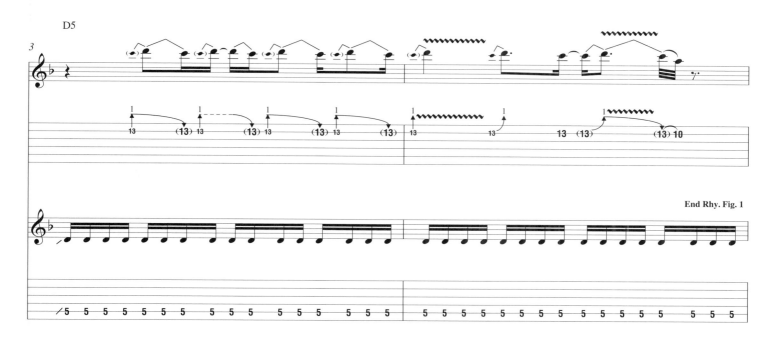

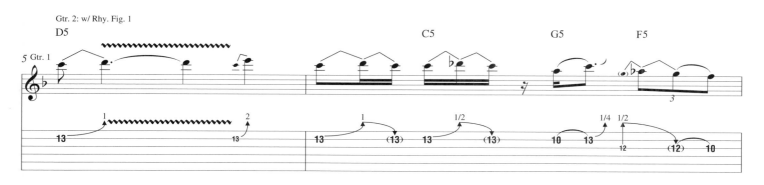

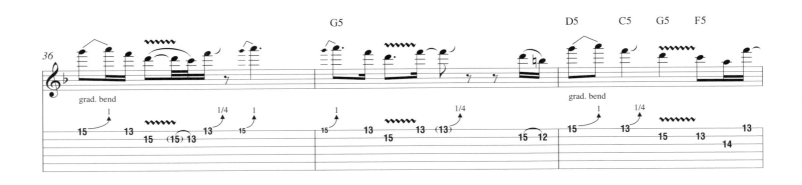

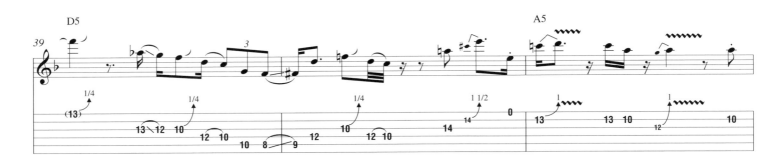

Gtr. 2: w/ Rhy. Fig. 2 (last 2 meas.)

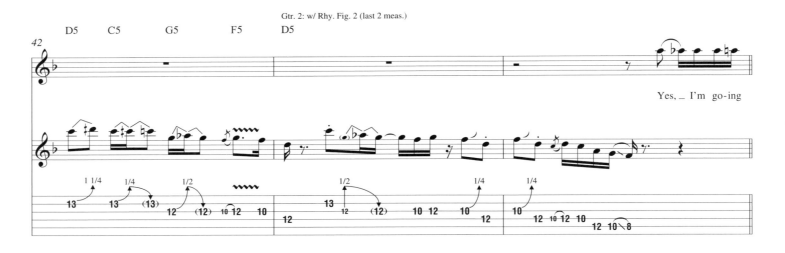

Yes, _ I'm go-ing

Chorus

Gtr. 2: w/ Rhy. Fig. 2

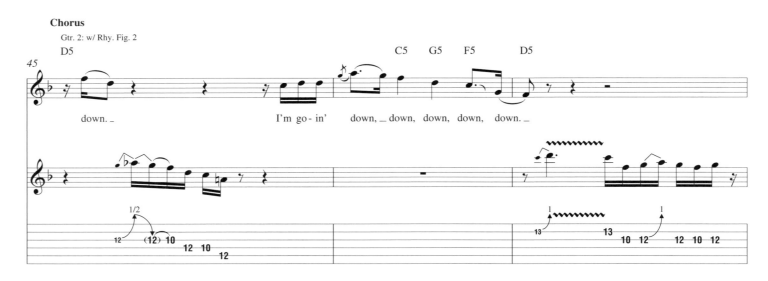

down. _

I'm go-in'   down, _ down, down, down, down. _

Outro-Guitar Solo

Gtr. 2: w/ Rhy. Fig. 2 (till fade)

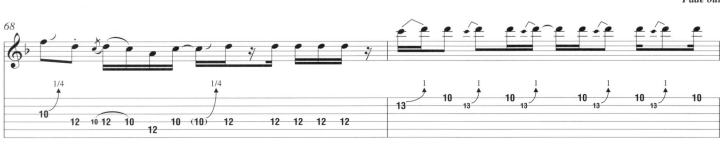

ESSENTIAL LICKS

Root Position Minor Pentatonic and Blues Scale

Freddie King, more than B.B., and in a manner markedly different from Albert, for example, raked the root and extension positions of the minor pentatonic, blues, and composite blues scales. He also played melodically within the major pentatonic scale via a fingering popular with blues, country, and rock guitarists.

Performance Tip: At their essence, blues guitar solos consist of a "string" of phrases that create tension through various means and ones that resolve the tension to the tonic, or root note, of the chord change. The following are a choice selection employed by King.

The figure below contains the root position of the C minor pentatonic scale, a favorite key for King, with the root (C) notes in white.

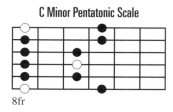

C Minor Pentatonic Scale

8fr

Lick 1

Lick 1 opens with the first three notes comprising "Blues Guitar 101." It satisfies several requirements for a blues classic: a quarter-tone bend on string 3, followed by notes (G and C) implying the harmony (C). The descending notes flowing next add the ♭7th (B♭) and end on a bend to the ♭5th (G♭) "blue note" for tension.

Lick 1

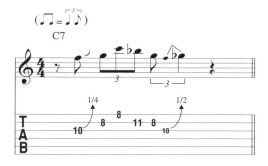

Performance Tip: Push off from string 3 with the ring finger and barre string 2–1 with the index finger (see photo).

Lick 2

A descending phrase, Lick 2 emphasizes the all-important ♭3rd (E♭) "blues note" on string 3 at fret 8 and generates tension like Lick 1.

Lick 2

Performance Tip: Bending the ♭3rd a quarter step is a time-honored blues tradition. Execute it by pulling *downward* with the index finger.

Lick 3

Even if played in a slow blues, Lick 3 requires the combination of strong index and ring fingers for the snappy pull-offs to the root (G) and 5th (D) notes. Simple in concept, it acknowledges the tonality (G and D) while adding the necessary blues "dirt" (B♭) and tension for a tasty fill or solo lick.

Lick 3

Lick 4

Lick 4 contains a harmonious one-step bend of the 4th (F) to the 5th (G) that closely follows the ♭7th (B♭) to imply the dominant seventh chord voicing (C7). Ending on the root (C) completes the tonality and resolution. Be aware how doubling the root adds dynamic punctuation to the conclusion of the lick and is a blues characteristic.

Lick 4

Performance Tip: Play the B♭ with the pinky and bend the F with the ring finger, backed by the middle and index fingers (see photo).

Lick 5

Lick 5 encapsulates the soloing concept of tension and release, or resolution, in one descending phrase. No matter the pitch, bends always create a certain amount of tension, whether less, as in the bend to the root (G) on string 2, or more, as in the bend of the 4th (C) to the 5th (D) on string 3. Naturally, resolution to the root occurs on string 4.

Lick 5

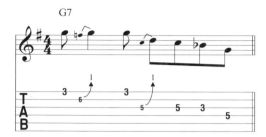

Performance Tip: Bend the F with the pinky, backed by the ring and middle. Bend the C with the ring finger, backed by the middle finger.

Albert King Box

After the root position of the minor pentatonic scale, King favored the extension, or "Albert King box."

Lick 6

Lick 6 satisfies the requirements for the "perfect" blues lick, as it establishes the G tonality with the root (G) note and ends with the classic ♭3rd (B♭) bent a quarter step to one of the two "true blue notes" in between it and the major 3rd (B).

Lick 6

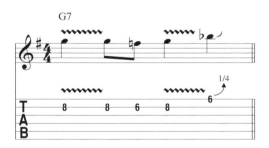

Performance Tip: Use the ring finger for the G note and the index finger for the F and B♭ notes. Push *upward* with the index to bend the B♭ (see photo).

Lick 7

Though any of the five positions of the minor pentatonic scale may be employed over the I, IV, or V chords, the extension position in Lick 7 contains certain attributes particularly relative to the IV chord. Hence, over the E♭ chord in the key of B♭, the root (E♭), ♭7th (D♭) bent a quarter step to the other "true blue note" in between the ♭7th and major 7th (D), and the 5th (B♭), complement the dominant tonality of the change.

Lick 7

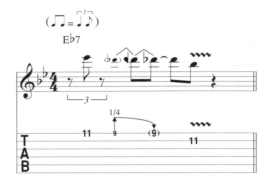

Performance Tip: Play the E♭ and the B♭ with the ring finger. Bend the D♭ with the index by pushing up and releasing (see photo).

Lick 8

Lick 8 is another dandy in the extension position designed to enhance the IV chord, this time in the key of G. As in Lick 7, it contains the root (C), 5th (G), and ♭7th (B♭) notes. However, by sustaining the ♭7th over beats 3–4, palpable anticipation is created towards the next measure.

Lick 8

Lick 9

Lick 9 also adds guts and a boost to the IV (G♭7) chord while featuring the cool King-ism of the "piggyback" bend, whereby he gradually goes up from a half step to a whole step. Always know that, when played over the IV chord, the ♭3rd of the I chord functions as the "leading tone" to confirm the tonality. The bend to the 9th (A♭), however, creates scintillating tension that anticipates the next measure of the I (D♭7) chord. Observe the F at fret 13 as a passing tone between E and G♭, producing a smooth, chromatic passage.

Lick 9

Performance Tip: As per usual, bend with the ring finger backed by the middle and index. Even with light-gauge strings (.010s, for example), you can see the wisdom of the backing fingers in order to best hold and control the slow bends.

Lick 10

When the root (D) is emphasized on string 2 at fret 15, the Albert King box does its duty as an important I (D7) chord scale position. Combined with the bend to the 5th (A) on beat 4, the D7 tonality is assured.

Lick 10

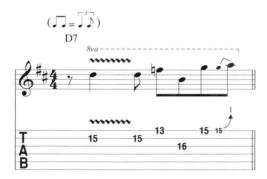

Performance Tip: Use the ring finger for the B note on string 3.

Composite Blues Scale

King tends to utilize the composite blues scale (Mixolydian mode plus blues scale) sparingly, but effectively.

Lick 11

Lick 11 is a prime example of how the major 3rd (E) from the Mixolydian mode and the ♭3rd (E♭) from the blues scale provide major-key emphasis and gritty blues tone, respectively.

Lick 11

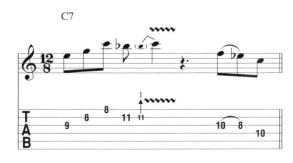

Performance Tip: On beat 1, slide silently into the E note on string 3 with the middle finger.

Lick 12

Lick 12 essentially reverses the order of the target notes seen in Lick 11. However, the ♭3rd is bent a quarter step to the "true blue note" in between the ♭3rd and major 3rd. Be aware how ending a phrase on the ♭7th over the I chord leads the ear directly to the next measure.

Lick 12

Performance Tip: Pull *downward* with the index finger on the ♭3rd, followed by the ring finger for the root (C) notes. Vibrato the ♭7th with the pinky in a rapid, fluttering motion by pulling *downward* in short bends to make it sing.

Lick 13

One of the many viable options afforded by the root position of the composite blues scale is the inclusion of the 6th (A) from the Mixolydian mode on string 2 to create a dramatic, descending melodic line: ♭7th–6th–5th. It can also encourage momentum as one travels down the scale on the way to resolution on the root on string 4.

Lick 13

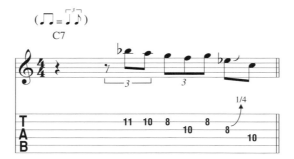

Performance Tip: Though King likely used his ring, middle, and index fingers on string 2, it is suggested to utilize the pinky, ring, and index for maximum efficiency. Plus, it is always better technically to be a four-finger, rather than a three-finger, soloist, despite the great accomplishments of proponents of the latter, such as King and his acolyte, Eric Clapton.

Lick 14

Lick 14 shows a different way to incorporate the 6th (E) on string 2 into a dynamic combination with the 5th (D) and ♭7th (F). With the inclusion of the major 3rd (B), the two most important blues target notes are accessed for an exceptionally rich blue mood.

Lick 14

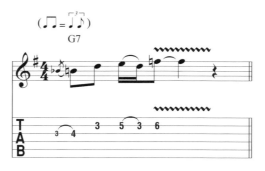

Performance Tip: As in Lick 13, utilize the index, ring, and pinky on string 2. Execute the vibrato with short, rapid bends by pulling *downward* with the pinky and strengthened by wrist motion for a slinky, serpentine effect.

Lick 15

The composite blues scale may also be used to great advantage for licks over the IV (D) chord. When analyzed melodically, the reason becomes crystal clear: the root (D), 2nd (E), 3rd (F♯), 5th (A), 6th (B), and ♭7th (C) are included.

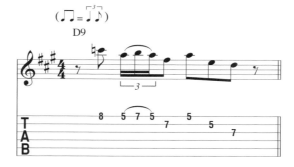

Performance Tip: Anchor the index finger on strings 2–1, using the ring finger for the notes at fret 7 on strings 3–1.

Lick 16

In Lick 16, be aware how notes from the composite blues scale may be bent at will as in the minor pentatonic or blues scales. Particularly effective over the I (A7) chord is a bend from the 2nd (B) to the major 3rd (C♯), as seen on beat 4.

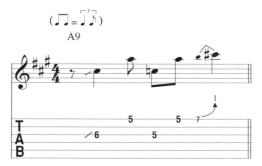

Performance Tip: After glissing into the fretted major 3rd on string 3 with the middle finger, barre strings 3–1 with the index finger for the root (A) and ♭3rd (C) notes. Bend the B with the ring finger, backed by the middle and index finger.

Lick 17

Lick 17 is a variation on the theme of Lick 16.

Performance Tip: Barre strings 2–1 with the index finger and bend the 2nd (D) to the 3rd (E) with the ring finger, backed up by the middle and index fingers.

Lick 18

More musical expression and information is packed into Lick 18 than some blues guitarists impart in a whole solo. The root (C), 2nd (D), 5th (G), 6th (A), and ♭7th (B♭) contribute to the C7 (I chord) tonality while the ♭3rd (E♭), bent a quarter step to the "true blue note," imparts the crucial spicy tang to the sumptuous blues stew.

Lick 18

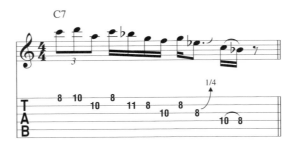

Performance Tip: In order to efficiently play the descending lick, and especially the 16th notes on beat 2, use the index finger as a guide at fret 8 on strings 1–4.

Lick 19

Due to its exceptional expressiveness, another bend from the 2nd (D) on string 1 appears in Lick 19, but for the duration of a luxurious one-and-a-half steps.

Lick 19

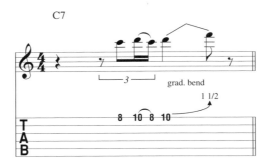

Performance Tip: Again, bend with the ring finger, backed by the middle and index, making sure to keep steady pressure against the fret.

Lick 20

A virtual tutorial on how the ♭3rd (E♭) and major 3rd (E), dynamically placed within a jam-packed riff in the root position of the composite blues scale, can help create a memorable, soul-searing lick.

Lick 20

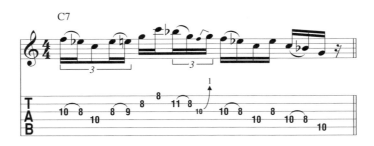

Performance Tip: The pull-offs from fret 10 to fret 8 on strings 3–4 should be accomplished with the ring and index fingers. On beat 2, bend the 4th (F) to the 5th (G) with the ring finger, backed by the middle and index, followed by the ring and index fingers for the pull-off.

Double Stops

Though King inserted few chords into his solos, he was quite fond of propulsive harmony provided by energetic, repetitive rhythms and bluesy double stops.

Lick 21

Lick 21 combines a classic E/C (5th/♭3rd) dyad from the A minor pentatonic or blues scale at the 12th position with descending dyads in 3rds from the A Mixolydian mode. Note that the C/A♭ (♭3rd/♭9th) dyad in measure 2 is a passing dyad that is not in the scale, but added to create a smooth (legato) effect.

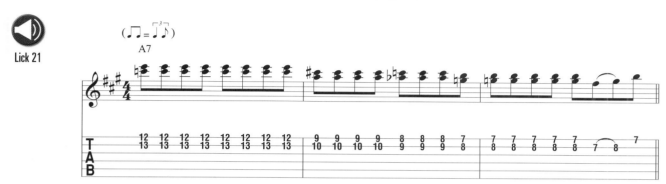

Performance Tip: Play all dyads with the middle and index fingers, low to high.

Lick 22

The G/E (♭7th/5th) dyad from the A Mixolydian mode in Lick 22 not only defines and emphasizes the A7 tonality, but the gradual relaxing of the phrasing from driving eighth notes to quarter notes helps ease the transition to the following measures (not shown), which contain single-note licks.

Performance Tip: Use your ring and index fingers, low to high.

Lick 23

Dyads in 3rds derived from the major scale, or Ionian mode, and voiced on strings 3–2 are a staple of electric blues guitar. Lick 23 provides a strong dose of major tonality and contains the type of "grace" dyad (on beat 1 and the "and" of beat 2) often used to impart the organic nature of the genre, wherein target notes, chords, or licks are approached from one fret below or above.

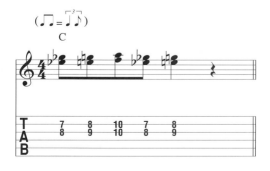

Performance Tip: Use the middle and index fingers, low to high, for the diagonal voicings and the ring finger as a small barre for A/F on beat 2.

Lick 24

Lick 24 combines dyads in 3rds from the E Mixolydian mode with a classic "train whistle" double stop from the seventh position of the E blues scale for a dramatic evocation of "blues power," emphasizing the IV (A7) chord. Observe the C#/A (3rd/root in the key of A) dyad paving the way to the ♭3rd (G) of E, which functions as the ♭7th of A7 to nail the dominant tonality.

Lick 24

Performance Tip: Use the ring and index, low to high, for D/B, followed by middle and index for C#/A. Maintain the fingering for the train whistle, executing the "true blue note" bend on string 2 with the middle finger.

King Comping

Freddie King was a shrewd, efficient rhythm guitarist whenever the opportunity presented itself.

Lick 25

Lick 25 features triple and double stops relative to D7 and E♭7 in stop time. In measure 1, the triple-stop implying a first-inversion (3rd on the bottom) D9 chord is as rich and hip a dominant voicing as one could want.

Lick 25

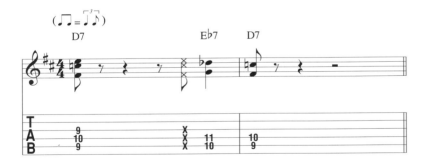

Performance Tip: Finger the triple stop as if playing an open-position D chord (see photo).

Lick 26

Lick 26 contains standard blues voicings from measure 12 of the final chorus of a 12-bar blues in F. The pitch ascends from the C bass note through the partial C7 barre chord to the jazzy F9 barre chord for dynamic effect.

Lick 26

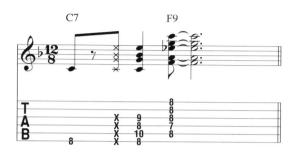

Performance Tip: Barre across all six strings with the index finger for the C7 chord, but be sure to strum just strings 6–3.

Lick 27

More hip dominant chords sit easily in the middle register so as not to get in the way of the other instruments or the vocals as they complement the swinging shuffle rhythm in Lick 27. Implying sixth and ninth chords, the voicings blend smoothly despite the difference in register.

Lick 27

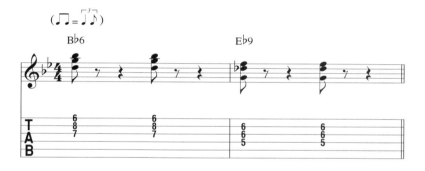

Performance Tip: For the B♭6 chord, use the middle, ring, and index fingers, low to high. For the E♭9, place the index on string 4 at fret 5 and barre strings 3–2 at fret 6 with the ring finger. If the ring finger happens to cover string 1, as well, stop the strum at string 2 for the proper execution of the chord.

Lick 28

King sometimes combined single-note licks with chords for a fluid transition to the harmony. Check out how the large interval leaps of the single notes add dynamics to the example, fitting for the last measure in a 12-bar blues song.

Lick 28

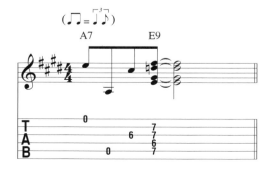

SIGNATURE RIFFS

Have You Ever Loved a Woman
From *Freddie King Sings,* 1961

The lyric content is probably a "duh" question for most men. King's disciple Eric Clapton could relate to it personally due to his dalliance in the '70s with Patti Boyd Harrison, who "belongs to your very best friend," and who is also the unrequited love object of his immortal masterpiece "Layla." A live version released on *E.C. Was Here* has ol' "Slowhand" ad-libbing "Should I mention any names?" after the line "she belongs to…"

The Texas Cannonball's slow blues classic is one of the few not penned by the guitarist. However, he invests the sensually languid groove with the most believable deep emotion in his vocal delivery and solo. The latter, in particular, packs in an amazing amount of musical expression in 12 concise measures, including the "fast change" from the I (C♯7) chord to the IV (F♯7) chord in measures 1–2, respectively.

Guitar Solo

Make no mistake, whether King is literally referencing a flesh and blood woman or not, the passion in his solo is as hot and real as it gets. So eager is he to let it flow that he gets a head start in measure 12 of verse 2 by jumping to the "Albert King box" in the C♯ composite blues scale and whomping down on the tonic note (C♯) over the V (G♯7) chord, where it functions as the 4th and creates musical tension. Resolving it, he bends the ♭3rd (E) a half step to the sweet major 3rd (E♯). It is here where King starts his seminar in dramatic blues phrasing by resting for three long beats before picking the root (C♯) note. In measure 2 (IV chord), he includes the root (F♯) while initiating one of his classic moves in the "Albert King box" of the C♯ composite blues scale. Using the C♯ on string 2 as "home base," he walks up E, E♯, and F♯ (♭7th, major 7th passing tone, and root of F♯) and repeats the phrase two more times in measure 3 (I chord), where the notes now function as the ♭3rd, major 3rd, and 4th of C♯. Whereas the sequence so far would appear to create tension and release, respectively, King is after bigger "game" since the anticipation made by the repetition of the repeated bends of the F♯ conspire to produce the first rush of dynamic energy in measures 1–4.

Dynamically, he relaxes the tension, taking a "breather" in measures 5–6 (IV chord) by gradually and gently descending down the extension and root positions of the scale while including emphasis on the consonant root and 5th (C♯) notes. Pacing himself and composing his improvisation as he goes along, he brilliantly references the beginning of his solo in measures 7–8 (I chord), resting for three dramatic beats in the former before subtly leading into the latter with G♯ (5th), B (♭7th), and C♯ (root) notes. The latter also contains a stuttering run up the root position of the C♯ blues scale, with the root played prominently several times to maintain focus on the I-chord tonality.

However, at the critical juncture of measure 9 (V chord), King produces sweet anticipation by bending D♯ (5th) to E♯ (6th). Be aware how virtually all 12-bar blues progressions peak in measure 9, as it is the first appearance of the V chord, and reverse direction down on the way to the I and V chords in measures 10–12. The bent and sustained C♯ (4th of G♯) creates tension into measure 10 (IV chord). There, King gets jazzy with the hip G (♭9th) and unusual E♯ (major 7th), the latter seemingly gleaned from the bebop dominant scale, making one wonder if he nicked the idea from one of his influences, jive sax man Louis Jordan (see Stylistic DNA).

F♯ Bebop Dominant Scale

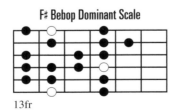

13fr

In a recommended technique, he ends on the C♯ (5th) in anticipation of the I chord in the turnaround (measure 11), where he again hits it on string 2 at fret 14. A classic run up the root position of the C♯ composite blues scale, including the major 3rd (E♯), resolves to the root (C♯). In measure 12, he cleverly ends two licks on the G♯. However, over beat 1 (I chord) it functions as the 5th, and over beat 2 (V chord) it becomes the root for conclusive resolution.

Performance Tip: On beats 3–4 of measure 10, walk down from G♯, G, and F♯ with the ring, middle, and index fingers. Shift the hand position down one fret and play the E♯ and F♯ with the index and middle fingers, respectively. This will leave the ring finger in an advantageous and efficient place to hit the C♯ on string 2 with the ring finger.

By the way: Depending on your point of view, this tale of taboo temptation has a happy ending, as King states in the last line of the lyrics: "Yes, 'cause there's something deep inside of you, won't let you wreck your best friend's home."

Have You Ever Loved A Woman
Guitar Solo

Guitar Solo
Slow Blues ♩. = 65

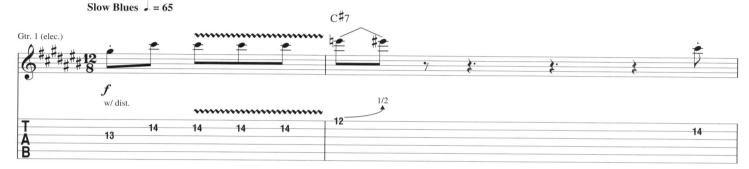

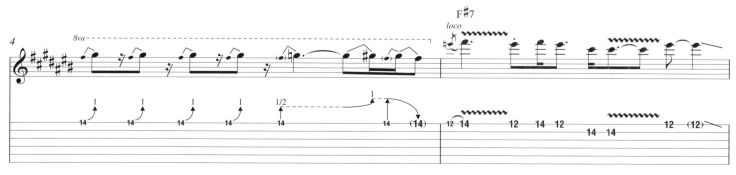

Hide Away
From *Let's Hide Away and Dance Away with Freddy King*, 1961

King was still known as "Freddy" in 1960, when, at his first session for King Records, he put to disk for posterity his future signature "calling card." He was upfront about acknowledging the various sources for the classic sections (noted below). "Hide Away" is unquestionably the #1 blues instrumental and so ubiquitous that music stores in Austin, Texas, are known to post a sign with the title of the song in a circle with a red line through it. It boogied and shuffled to #5 and #29 on the R&B and pop singles charts, respectively, and has been covered countless times by blues pickers looking to show their cred. By far the most famous and worthy is the one by Eric Clapton, which appeared on the first Bluesbreakers album in 1967.

The arrangement consists of seven 12-bar choruses, labeled as Sections A–G. It is a literal blues smorgasbord—or, in contemporary vernacular, a brilliant mashup of blues forms—as the sequence builds and evolves dramatically and dynamically with intuitive logic. Because each section is so distinct and valuable, all will be discussed. In particular, the song is a terrific example of the way the major pentatonic scale can be utilized for melodic riffs when the minor pentatonic or blues scale might be too abrasive and dissonant.

Sections A and B

The open-string signature riffs are acknowledged as originating from "Hound Dog's Boogie" by Hound Dog Taylor. Harmonicist Shakey Jake claimed that he and Magic Sam "stole" it from Taylor, and King "stole" it from them when he lived and gigged in the Midwest blues mecca, Chicago. The title comes from Mel's Hide Away Lounge, a popular West Side blues joint in the '50s and '60s. As one of the most recognizable riffs in the blues, it kicks off the pickup measure and measure 1 of Section A. It is derived from the open position of the E major pentatonic scale, as are measures 2, 4, 6, and 8–10, and similar measures in Sections B (and G). Observe how the B (open string 2), C#, and E (open string 1) notes serve to harmonize equally with the I (E) and IV (A) chords as the 5th, 6th, and root and 2nd, 3rd, and 5th, respectively. Notice how King skillfully inserts open-string boogie patterns for the I and IV chords in measures 1, 3, 5, and 7, proving his unsurpassed tenure as the reigning blues trio guitarist, despite the sympathetic and supportive comping of blues pianist Sonny Thompson on the original recording. Of prime importance is his editing of the boogie patterns when the major pentatonic licks overlap with the rhythm riffs by crossing bar lines in order to maintain the musical *illusion* of two guitarists playing simultaneously.

Be sure to check out how the turnaround (measures 11–12) is constructed from the open position of the E minor pentatonic scale following crucial resolution to the tonic chord on beat 1 of measure 11 via a hammer-on to the major-tonality-defining major 3rd (G#). In addition, after further complementing the E7 change in measure 11 with the root (E), 5th (B), and ♭7th (D) notes, King dissects a broken B7 chord with his unique sense of blues expression. The inclusion of the D#/B (3rd/root) dyad contributes harmonic weight among the single notes surrounding it.

Performance Tip: Forget the "one-finger-per-fret" system of fingering in measures 1–10. Instead, hammer the C# on string 2 at fret 2 with the strong middle finger and gliss from F# to G# on string 1 with the same finger. In addition, use it for the triplet hammer-ons in measures 4, 8, and 10.

Hide Away
Section A

Moderate Shuffle ♩ = 134

Gtr. 1 (elec.)

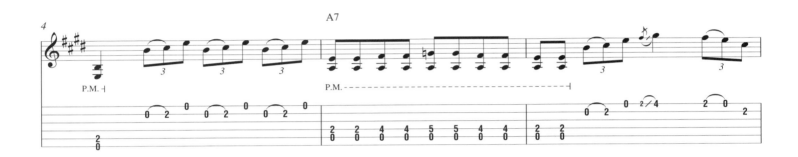

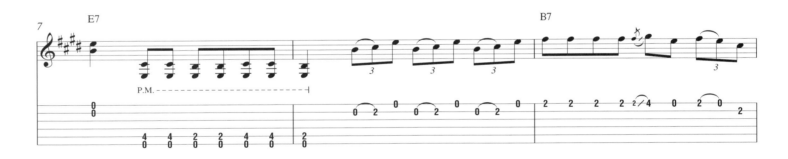

Hide Away
Section B

Section C

Section C, "snitched" from the signature bass line riffs in Jimmy McCracklin's "The Walk" (1958), is derived from the indispensable composite blues scale relative to each chord change, producing dynamic contrast, both in syncopation and register, to Sections A and B.

Performance Tip: Hammer from the middle finger to the ring finger for the G to G# move on string 6 and the C to C# move on string 5 for the I (E7) and IV (A7) chords, respectively. The hand will now be in the most efficient position for accessing the notes on strings 5 and 4 for the I and IV changes, respectively, with the index, pinky, index, ring, and index fingers. For the V (B7) chord, gliss into fret 6 with the ring finger and execute the line of notes on string 4 with the same fingers as the other changes.

Hide Away
Section C

Section D

The I and IV changes in measures 1–8 are similar to verse 2 of "Guitar Boogie" (1948) by Arthur "Guitar Boogie" Smith. Many similar versions followed Smith's, including "Guitar Boogie Shuffle" (1959) by bassist Frank Virtue and the Virtues with Jimmy Bruno, Sr. on lead guitar. The rolling pattern essentially incorporates the major triad notes of the root, 3rd, and 5th relative to E and A. Of course, the major 3rd is preceded by the ♭3rd as a "grace note" in what is an organic move from "Blues Guitar 101." Measures 9–10 (V and IV chords), however, contain a walking bass line relative to each chord change, heretofore not seen in "Hide Away" or any other Freddie King tune. The most distinguishing feature is the way the major pentatonic line (save for the ubiquitous ♭3rd grace note in measure 10) ascends and descends dynamically within the span of a measure. Continuing in a similar vein, King walks up the E composite blues scale in measure 11 with a bass line. Producing anticipation for the B target note is the wise employment of the chromatic notes G (♭3rd), G♯ (3rd), A (4th), and B♭ (♭5th), followed by A and B (5th). Measure 12, logically enough, resolves with finality to an open-position B7 chord.

Performance Tip: The pick hand is the "driving wheel" in measures 1–10. For maximum blues power, use strict alternate (down-up-down-up, etc.) pick strokes.

Section E

With a nod to the jazzy side of Robert Junior Lockwood, in measures 1–2, King utilizes an exceptionally hip E9 voicing—a third-inversion voicing with the ♭7th (D) as the bottom note—to highlight the dramatic stop-time and climactic moment of "Hide Away." Here are all the inversions:

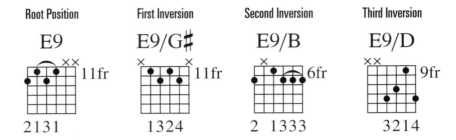

Root Position	First Inversion	Second Inversion	Third Inversion
E9	E9/G♯	E9/B	E9/D
11fr	11fr	6fr	9fr
2131	1324	2 1333	3214

Inversions, along with other alternate chord voicings, are especially valuable in the blues, where they lend welcome variety to common and predictable I–IV–V progressions.

Along with the propulsive, descending 6ths derived from the E Mixolydian mode in measures 3–4, the E9 constitutes the most copped aspect of the tune. Adding to the musical drama are measures 5–8, where the IV and I changes are harmonized as accompaniment with the punchy bass string boogie patterns seen in Sections A, B, and G. Likewise, King repeats the major pentatonic riffs and turnaround similar to those found in measures 9–12 of Sections A and B.

Performance Tip: Access the E9 with the ring, middle, index and pinky fingers, low to high. Do not despair over the unusual two-fret span between the middle and index fingers on strings 3 and 2, respectively, if it is a stretch at first! Go slowly and gently until it can be accomplished easily and quickly.

Hide Away
Section E

Section F

King shamelessly appropriated the bluesy signature riff from the theme song of the popular 1958–61 TV detective show *Peter Gunn*. Whereas the original composition is a I-chord (F) modal caper, King expanded the riff to fit within his 12-bar blues framework by incorporating the IV (A) chord, as well. However, he deviated for the V (B) chord in measure 9 by merely thumping the root (B) note in a driving eighth-note rhythm. Also note the change to a straight-eighth feel here, quickly dropped at the end of the Section for the return to the main shuffled theme in Section G. Henry "Hank" Mancini, the famous composer also known for the *Pink Panther* theme, among many others, built his world-famous riff from the F composite blues scale.

Performance Tip: Utilize the index and middle fingers for the I and IV chord patterns, employing the index finger for the notes at frets 2 and 4, and the middle finger for frets 3 and 5.

Hide Away
Section F

Section G

With a few insignificant differences, Section G is very similar to Sections A and B, save for the turnaround (measures 11–12). Shifting to the open position of the composite blues scale, King walks down string 1 and then up to an implied E major chord (the G#/E [3rd/root] dyad) in measure 12.

Performance Tip: Start with the middle finger on the G note at fret 3 in measure 11, followed by the index finger for the F# (string 1) and C# (string 2). Walk up with the index, middle, and ring fingers. Take a quick breather while snapping the open first and second strings and reset the hand position in order to access the dyad with the middle and index fingers, low to high. Check out the way that the dyad is sustained languorously into bar 13 as a means to wind down, rather than end abruptly.

Hide Away
Section G

Butterscotch (Onion Rings)
From *Let's Hide Away and Dance Away with Freddy King*, 1961

King reportedly was often miffed at the seemingly cavalier titles King/Federal Records owner Syd Nathan bestowed on his instrumentals, only picking a couple himself. "Butterscotch" was originally called "Onion Rings" and was recorded on the same amazingly productive day as "Sen-Sa-Shun," "Side Tracked," "The Stumble," "San-Ho-Zay," "Wash Out," "Just Pickin'," and "Heads Up" in the spring of 1961. It was released as the B-side of "Now I've Got a Woman."

Section A

"Butterscotch" consists of Sections A–H, with Section C functioning as a dynamic 8-bar bridge among the 12-bar sections. The main 12-bar theme put forth in Section A is similar to Sections B, D, G, and H (not shown) and is deceptively simple. In classic blues style, it features call and response, with measures 1, 3, 7, and 11 (I chord), as well as measure 5 (IV chord), representing the call via a bouncy riff derived from the C Mixolydian mode in third position. Naturally, the riff in measure 5 moves up a set of strings to include notes relative to the F Mixolydian mode. Observe the way that the octave jump on beats 1–2 of the I and IV changes boosts the forward motion of the riff due to the span of the interval.

In measures 2, 4, and 8 (C7 chord), as well as in measure 6 (F7 chord), King seamlessly shifts to the third-position C minor pentatonic scale, commanding it to do his improvisational bidding for the response. Pay close attention to and internalize how he uses virtually the same minimal number notes for both the I and IV change. Of particular importance is the way the E♭ (string 2, fret 4) functions as the gritty ♭3rd of C7 and the ♭7th of F7. The concept of relying on the changing harmony to alter the same melody notes occurs in many styles of music, but is of special significance in the blues and related genres given the emphasis on the unsurpassed importance of I–IV changes.

As has been previously pointed out and will continue to be throughout this in-depth exploration of the art of the electric blues guitar as exemplified by Freddie King, his improvisational phrasing is unexcelled. The response measures again prove the bold claim as he swings away with graceful execution that is enhanced by numerous triplets.

Performance Tip: Section A is a mini-tutorial in subtle, nuanced bending. Use the index finger to pull *down* on the quarter-step "blue notes" (B♭ [♭7th] on string 3 in measures 1, 3, 7, and 11). The one-step bends from F (4th) to G (5th) in measures 2, 4, 6, and 8 should be approached with the ring finger, backed by the middle and index, with the index poised to play the E♭ at fret 4. Pay strict attention to the phrasing of the buttery one-step bends in measures 2 and 8, which benefit greatly from the strength and control provided by the three-finger technique.

Butterscotch
Section A

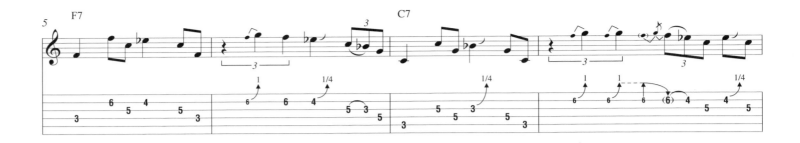

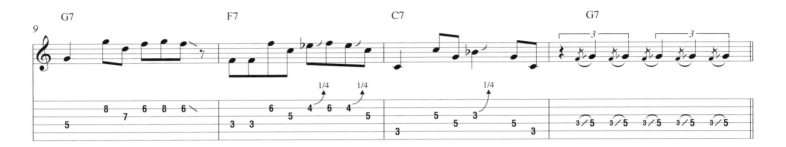

Section C

For Freddie King, measure 2 contains an unusual combination of notes on strings 1–2, plucked from the F composite blues scale.

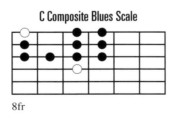

F Composite Blues Scale

The result is a memorable, liltingly melodic phrase featuring not only the typical root (F) and ♭3rd (A♭), but the 2nd (or 9th, G) and 6th (D), expressing a lyrical, upbeat feel as opposed to the more common gritty, "down home" ambience often associated with the blues. Observe how measures 3–4 (I chord) contain a similar lick drawn from the C composite blues scale as King again displays his expansive improvisational skills by intelligently changing keys like a jazz man.

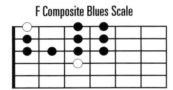

C Composite Blues Scale

8fr

Performance Tip: Be sure to employ the pinky and ring fingers along with the index when playing the three-note combinations on strings 1–2.

Butterscotch
Section C

C

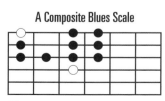

Sen-Sa-Shun
From *Let's Hide Away and Dance Away with Freddy King*, 1961

Also known as "Bumble Bee Sting," the instrumental "Sen-Sa-Shun" bears a resemblance to "San-Ho-Zay," which was cut the same day.

Section A

If there is one over-riding concept to be learned from "Sen-Sa-Shun," it is the way the exact same combination of notes may be repeated to harmonize acceptably over the I and IV chords, and even the V chord, in a blues progression. As mentioned in Section A of "Butterscotch," the changing harmony has the significant effect of making the licks, riffs, or melodies appear to be changing, as well. Measures 1–2 (I chord) and 5–6 (IV chord) prove the point admirably as the hip triple and double stops work their musical magic. Though it may have been a coincidence, the riffs sound remarkably like the vocal melody of "Got My Mojo Working."

Dig the raunchy, gritty blues sound of the C/G/E♭ (♭3rd/♭7th/♭5th) triple stop, which is highly unusual for the key of A. Appearing in the pickup measure and measure 2 (A7), it opens the tune with a clanging wake-up call! In measures 1, 5, and 6, it is reduced to a double stop in order to combine with two other dyads on strings 3–2 to create a fat, melodic line derived from the A composite blues scale.

A Composite Blues Scale

5fr

Observe the ♭5th (E♭) on string 3 at fret 8 from the blues scale, which is included to create a double stop on strings 3–2 at fret 8. The figures below show the double-stop combinations on strings 2–1 and 3–2 frequently seen in blues and rockabilly music.

Double-Stop Combinations

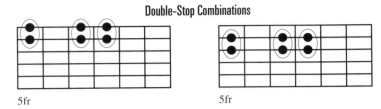

Performance Tip: Slide into the triple stop with the index finger. Use the ring finger as a small barre for the double stops at both frets 8 and 7, with the index playing the ones at fret 5.

Sen-Sa-Shun
Section A

Section C

It cannot be stressed too many times how versatile and efficient the extension position ("Albert King box") of the minor pentatonic scale can and should be as a prime improvisational tool.

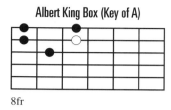

Albert King Box (Key of A)

8fr

See how King employs it in measures 1–10. Pay particular attention to the half-step bend from D to E♭ (snarky ♭5th) on string 1 at fret 10 in measures 4–9 against the I (A7), IV (D7), and V (E7) changes, where it elicits a different effect with each.

Performance Tip: With few exceptions, utilize the index finger on fret 8 and the ring finger on fret 10.

Sen-Sa-Shun
Section C

Section D

Again displaying one of the most important tenets of dynamic blues guitar, King repeats a one-measure riff virtually identically in measures 1–11. Derived from the A composite blues scale on strings 6–5, it basically repeats the open sixth string (E), the F♯ at fret 2 of string 6, and the open fifth string (A). However, check out the kicker—the ♭3rd (C) on string 5 at fret 3 on beat 4 of each measure—for the bluesy spice mixed in with the three harmonious notes.

Sen-Sa-Shun
Section D

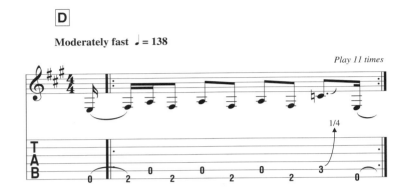

Performance Tip: Play the F♯ with the middle finger and the C with the ring finger. More importantly, due to the brisk tempo, employ alternate (down-up-down-up, etc.) picking strokes until the C note, which should also be picked with a downstroke.

Side Tracked
From *Let's Hide Away and Dance Away with Freddy King*, 1961

The list of Freddie King disciples who recorded versions of this swinging instrumental classic is a "Who's Who" of blues guitar luminaries, including Bugs Henderson, Hollywood Fats, Tinsley Ellis, Jeff Golub, Anson Funderburgh, and Stan Webb from Chicken Shack, the British blues band, among others.

Section B

The adjective "brilliant" cannot be tossed around too often when Freddie King is involved. Section B, or the main theme, is a prime example, as he commands hip dyads relative to the I (G) and IV (C9) chords upon which to construct a solid, harmonious blues façade. For the G, it is F/D (♭7th/5th), and for C9, it is E/C (3rd/root), as first seen in measures 1–2, respectively, where they function as the call in the call and response scheme. The sheer repetition of the notes engenders musical tension and anticipation to the response revealed in measures 3–4 and 7–8 (I chord), featuring melodious runs in the root position of the G composite blues scale.

Be aware that the dyads are gleaned from the G Mixolydian mode.

Side Tracked
Example 1

However, the main lesson to be learned is the way King wisely chooses the dyads to represent the changes. The E/C for the IV (C9) chord is a no-brainer, but "picking" F/D to precede it for the I chord makes for a most memorable combination.

Performance Tip: Play the signature dyad for the I chord with the ring and index fingers, low to high. For the IV chord, use the middle and index fingers, low to high. Use strict alternate picking in each measure, starting with a downstroke. However, be aware of the necessary shift on beat 3 of the IV chord, where the ring finger should quickly gliss up to fret 5 (G) on string 4 while maintaining precise picking.

Just Pickin'
From *Let's Hide Away and Dance Away with Freddy King*, 1961

It is reasonable to assume Buddy Guy was inspired to write "Mary Had a Little Lamb" in 1968 after hearing the Freddie King instrumental. While the Guy version takes its unusual lyric cue from the classic children's nursery rhyme, King was…"Just Pickin'." It was released as the B-side of "Come On."

Section A

Similar to many of his other instrumentals, King likewise constructed it with call and response in mind. Measures 1, 3, 5, and 7 function as the call via alternating licks from the E and A composite blues scales, respectively. Measures 2, 4, 6, and 8 are the response and contain chords for the IV (A7) and I (E7) chords (measures 2 and 4, respectively) and implied chords for the V (B7) chord (measure 6) and the I chord (measure 8). Observe how having the call on the bass strings and the response on the treble strings contribute a dynamic effect, as well as suggesting two different "voices" or guitarists.

Performance Tip: In measure 1, play the C on string 5 with the middle finger and hammer onto the C♯ with the ring finger. It will place the hand in the best position to follow with the index finger on the E on string 4. Freddie likely used his ring finger instead of his pinky for the bent G notes on string 4, but he also had large hands to accommodate the stretch. Using the pinky is recommended.

Just Pickin'
Section A

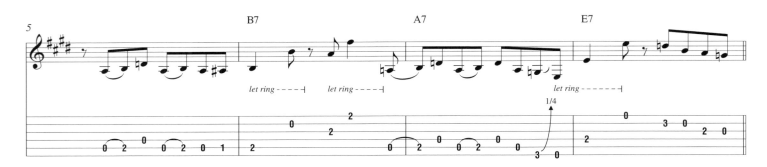

Section C

King shows how to do more with less by restricting himself to the root octave position of the E minor pentatonic scale and exercising his superb sense of phrasing. The "secret" of his success is the way he jumps over adjacent strings, in particular the octave leap of E to E, creating wider intervals than the usual standard blues licks, thus creating bouncy, upbeat patterns. Be cognizant that the riffs in each measure are virtually identical, with the crucial note being the last one, E, save for the one in measure 4, which hangs on the G until measure 5, resolving to the root (B) of the V (B7) chord.

It cannot be stressed too many times how the right combination of notes, particularly from the stripped-down minor pentatonic scale, can be repeated over the I, IV, and V chords in the blues and blues-based music to produce a memorable motif like the ones invented by King.

Performance Tip: Quite simply, only the index and ring fingers are required for the riffs. The only potentially challenging move is from the E on string 1 to the G on string 3 at fret 12, which could be accomplished solely with the index finger in a brisk lateral motion. You could also try barring the index over the top three strings at fret 12 by fretting the E with the index knuckle and "rolling" it over to catch the G with the index tip.

Just Pickin'
Section C

In the Open
From *Let's Hide Away and Dance Away with Freddy King*, 1961

The A-side of "I'm on My Way to Atlanta," "In the Open" is arguably one of the most challenging King instrumentals due to the quick and seamless blending of full dominant chords and classic licks in a brisk call and response. One of the few followers of the Texas powerhouse capable of covering it, and a fellow Lone Star virtuoso, Stevie Ray Vaughan included it in a live radio broadcast from Austin in 1980. In 1992, it was released on *In the Beginning* with bassist Jackie Newhouse, who preceded Tommy Shannon in Double Trouble.

Section A

Over a steady, driving "surf rock beat," King composes brilliantly in 24 measures formed by doubling the standard I–IV–V 12-bar changes. Right off, he "announces" the originality of his instrumental composition by flashing an ominous-sounding A9 voicing for his I chord. Essentially, it is a typical first-inversion ninth chord favored by T-Bone Walker and others.

Section A functions as the "head" of the tune. A term likely originating in instrumental jazz, it refers to a composed melody, motif, or series of riffs tied to the chord changes that may repeat twice before improvisation takes place over the changes, and is often reprised at the end of the song.

King comps syncopated ninth chord voicings in the odd-numbered measures and crackling licks from the root position of the A minor pentatonic scale in the even measures. Observe the way no two licks are exactly alike. This is crucial to the musical expression and especially important in regard to phrasing. At the same time, be aware of the measures in which King varies the last note of each lick, as opposed to repeating the root for resolution as in measures 2, 4, 6, and 14 (I chord). For a prime example, in measures 11–12, he sustains a note with a gradual bend across the bar line by leaving out a strum of the D9 chord on beat 4 (measure 11). In measure 8 (I chord), he ends on C (♭3rd), anticipating the D9 (IV chord) harmony in measure 9, where it functions as the ♭7th. In measure 12 (IV chord), King ends on the A note at fret 7 of string 4, anticipating the I (A9) chord in measure 13. Likewise, in measure 18 (V chord), he finishes on the open fourth string (D), emphasizing the dominant quality of E9 while preceding and previewing the IV (D) chord in measure 19. Also of significance is the bend on string 3, which appears in almost every improvised measure. The example below contains the basic version of this most classic and versatile of blues licks.

In the Open
Example 1

Performance Tip: Access the A9 chord with the index, ring, middle, and pinky fingers, low to high. Or you can use the three-finger version (that Freddie probably used) by barring the index across the 4th fret for (low to high): index, middle, index, ring.

In the Open
Section A

A

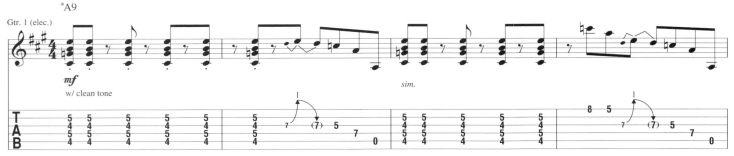

*Chord symbols reflect overall harmony.

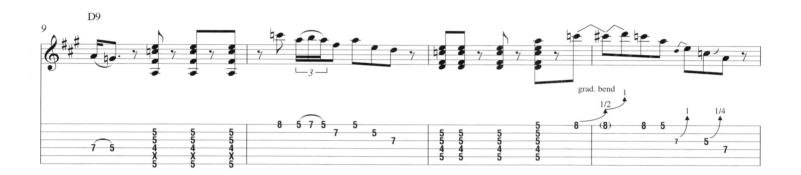

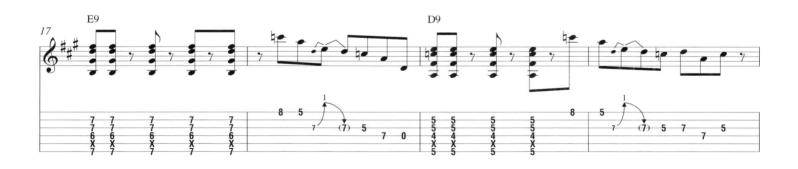

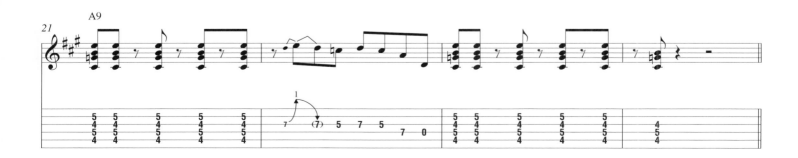

Funnybone
From *Freddy King Gives You a Bonanza of Instrumentals*, 1965

King brought his backlog of country blues licks to bear on a dance rhythm popular at the time in such fads as the Twist, the Watusi, and the Hully Gully, among others. Recording it was no doubt encouraged by King/Federal Records head honcho Syd Nathan, who was wise to pop culture trends. As "Sen-Sa-Shun" was a variation on "San-Ho-Zay," "Funnybone" is a variation on "Just Pickin'." The latter two also bear a passing resemblance to the classic "Come On" by Earl King from 1960.

Section A

As was regularly his wont, King arranged his easy-grooving instrumental in his preferred call and response mode. Hence, following the pickup call, the 12 bars of Section A alternate measures of trebly, exceptionally minimal response notes and the call of chords or chordal indicators. In measures 1–8, the former literally consist of just the ♭7th (D) of E7 (I chord) and the ♭7th (G) of A7 (IV chord) in conjunction with the open sixth string (E) and open fifth string (A), played once each. The response is mainly a series of pull-offs from E to D (open fourth string) in second position for the I chord, except for measure 4, where the ♭3rd (G) on string 6 is bent a quarter step to the hip "true blue note" in between the ♭3rd and major 3rd (G♯), preceding the open fifth string of the IV chord in measure 5. The V (B7) chord in measure 9 breaks with the system and contains a broken open-position B7 chord.

Know and learn the way King uses the effective dynamics of contrasting bass and treble notes to imply a bigger sound, inasmuch as the ear tends to fill in the sonic void in the midrange. The importance is not to be easily dismissed, especially as so many contemporary rock and blues guitarists feel the need to fill every musical nook and cranny by overplaying.

Performance Tip: Use the strong middle finger for the pull-offs and the B note in the pickup measure, as well as in measures 2, 6, and 8.

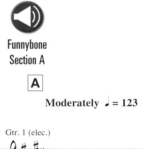

Funnybone
Section A

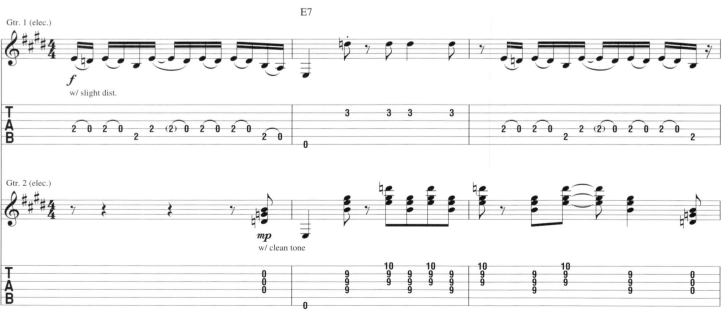

Section C

King inserts a funky eight-measure bridge after Section B (similar to A, but not shown) accompanied only by the drums. The entire I–IV–V progression consists of syncopated bass notes on strings 5–6 gleaned from the E minor pentatonic scale and carefully selected to follow the chord changes, with resolution on the appropriate root note. Again, King demonstrates in action the value of the "less is more" philosophy behind "Funnybone."

Performance Tip: All bends should be executed by pulling down with either the index or ring finger.

Funnybone
Section C

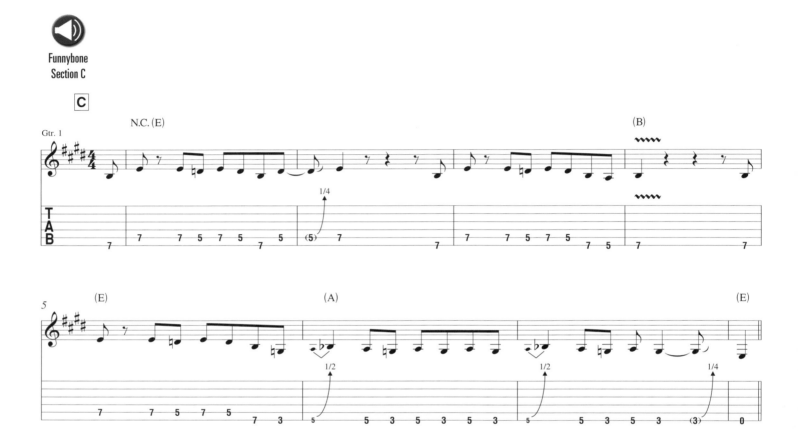

The Sad Nite Owl
From *Freddy King Gives You a Bonanza of Instrumentals*, 1965

"The Sad Nite Owl" is a rare Freddie King slow-blues instrumental. Less well-known than Cannonball Adderley's 1966 jazzy R&B classic "Mercy, Mercy, Mercy," but every bit as evocative of a smoky after-hours joint with the lights down low, the air thick with the waft of alcohol and melancholy.

Section A

More than most postwar electric blues guitarists, King employed dyads to add sumptuous harmony to several of his famous instrumentals. In the "The Sad Nite Owl," two guitars are employed to harmonize the dyads, played entirely in 3rds.

Be sure to see the organic half-step moves to the dyads containing the tonality-defining 3rd/5th or 3rd/root in the pickup measure and in measures 1, 4, 5, 8, 9, 10, and 11, producing a subtle, propulsive effect. Measures 3–4 and 7–8 (I chord) contain a stunning two-measure phrase derived from the G composite blues scale that ascends and descends gracefully.

After checking out each individual guitar part, try playing both guitar parts together with adjacent-string dyads. Here is the G Mixolydian mode played in 3rds:

The Sad Nite Owl
Example 1

The Sad Nite Owl
Section A

Palace of the King
From *Getting Ready...*, 1971

The first of his three albums for Leon Russell's Shelter Records ushered in the last chapter of Freddie King's career while helping to introduce him to a newer, younger rock audience. The mythically biographical "Palace of the King" was written by Donald "Duck" Dunn from Booker T & the MGs, Don Nix, and Russell, and is a rousing, funky blues-rock anthem covered by many guitarists, including John Mayall, Leslie West, John Mayer, Brian Lee, and Kenny Wayne Shepherd, among others.

Intro and Verse 1

Funk was often the order of the day in the '70s, even in the blues world. The intro and verses contain a cool, repetitive, two-measure syncopated signature riff composed of a thumping bass pattern on the low E string derived from the E major pentatonic scale, and a tart triple stop that, in another context, could imply an Em7 tonality or even a G major triad. Here, however, it imparts a quick hit of blues-approved musical tension in measure 1 of the phrase, which is resolved to the root (E) note in measure 2.

Performance Tip: Use the pinky and index fingers for the bass line and smack the triple stop with a small ring-finger barre.

Palace of the King
Intro and Verse 1

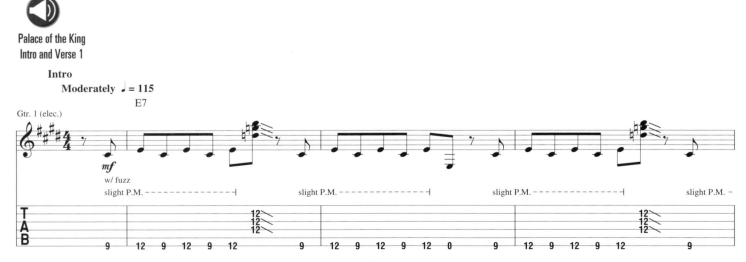

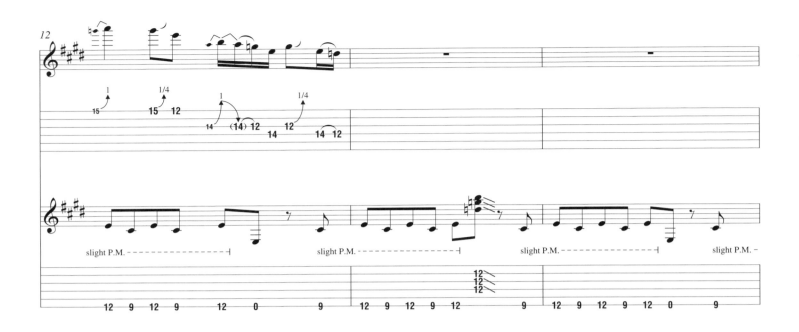

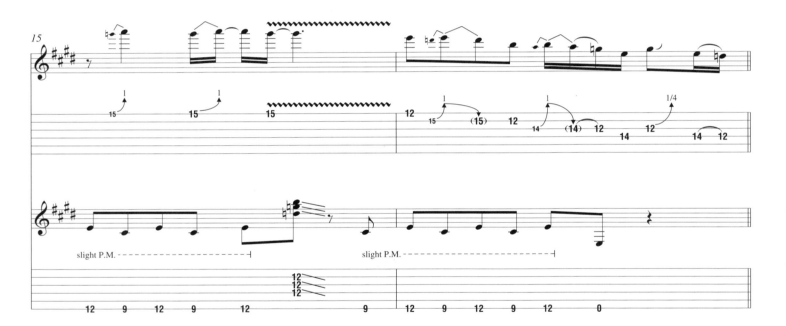

Pack It Up
From *Burglar*, 1974

Produced, in part, by legendary British producer Mike Vernon, the album reached #53 on the R&B charts with a selection of choice material contributed by a number of composers and featuring a slew of honored guests, including Eric Clapton and the American musicians who backed him in Derek and the Dominos. "Pack It Up" was written and originally performed in 1974 by the sprawling British funk group Gonzalez with George Chandler on lead vocals.

Intro

The intro is pure '70s funk guitar as proffered by British rhythm guitarist Bobby Tench (Gtr. 1), who previously played with Gonzalez, as well as the Jeff Beck Group and others. Born out of classic James Brown funk from the '60s featuring the legendary pioneer "funkateer" Jimmy Nolen, the signature riff involves a deceptively simple line from the root position of the F Mixolydian mode, voiced on string 4.

Performance Tip: Obviously, the index and ring fingers would be the most logical choice for the riff, but the heart of the matter is the phrasing and "stinky" syncopation. (**Note:** The term "funk" is a historically African-American word originally referring to a foul, unhygienic body odor. In time, it became slang for something "earthy" and the essence of physical reality. Though it was applied previously to some blues and jazz, it became synonymous with the post-1964 music of James Brown, which is so rhythmically, melodically, and harmonically primal.) Play all downstrokes, except on beat 4, where a down-up pattern is most efficient.

Pack It Up
Intro

*Chord symbols reflect implied harmony.

Guitar Solo: Riff A

Tench (Gtr. 1) provides more funk under King's slashing solo with a two-measure, horn-like line (Riff A) derived from the root position of the F minor pentatonic scale, with the E (major 7th) on string 4 at fret 2 functioning as a passing tone. So cool and expertly composed, it could function as the basis of an entire song.

Performance Tip: Be sure to hit the A♭ (♭3rd) on string 6 at fret 4 with the pinky, bending *downward* to the "true blue note."

Pack It Up
Guitar Solo/Riff A

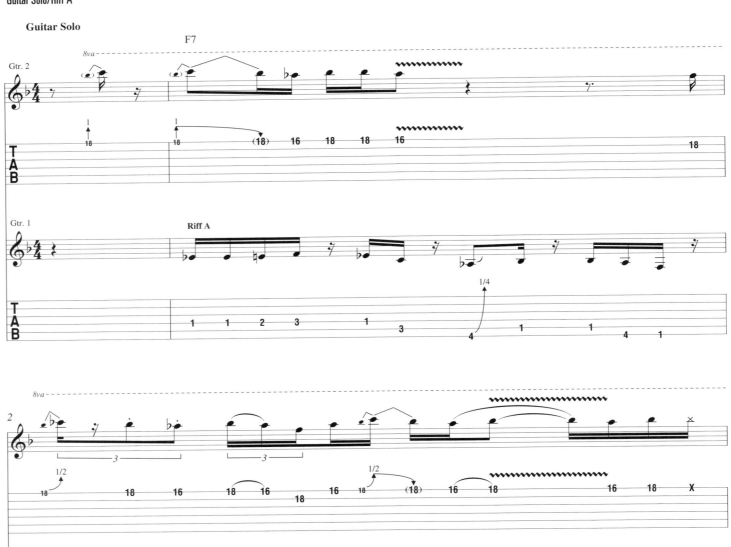

INTEGRAL TECHNIQUES

Picking

By picking single-note lines extensively with an upstroke via his metal index fingerpick, King produced an exceptionally biting, aggressive attack when desired. Most guitarists, however, will opt for a plastic flatpick and, with a change of direction from the usual preponderance of downstrokes, an equally exciting sound may be realized. Below is an especially effective, piercing example due to the high register. Observe how picking upward on string 1 allows for extra force and a more exaggerated, even theatrical, motion!

Techniques
Example 1

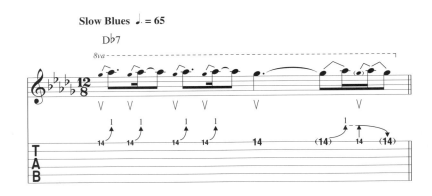

Performance Tip: Bend with the ring finger, backed by the middle and index.

Double stops on strings 2–1 will clang like a fire bell when banged with sharp upstrokes.

Techniques
Example 2

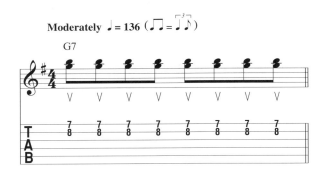

Performance Tip: Use more wrist, and less forearm, to avoid accidentally striking string 3.

Amazingly, King would use all upstrokes, even on patterns like the one below.

Techniques
Example 3

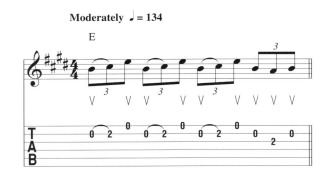

Though alternate downstrokes and upstrokes with the flatpick would be more efficient, all upstrokes will make for the required snappy attack.

Performance Tip: A slight tilting of the pick towards the open second string will help ensure clean execution (see photo).

If nothing else, this next example will build wrist strength!

Techniques
Example 4

Performance Tip: Use all upstrokes, including the D note on string 2 at fret 15.

In the example below, King likely would have used his metal index fingerpick on string 4 and his plastic thumbpick on string 5, alternating upstrokes and downstrokes.

Techniques
Example 5

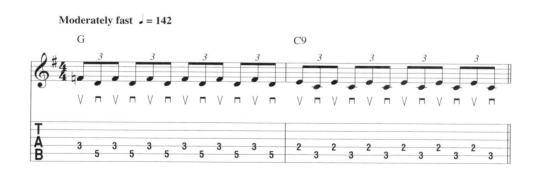

Performance Tip: With just a flatpick, employ the same, efficient up-down system as King.

Bending

Bending the ♭3rd a quarter step to the "true blue note" is a time-honored blues guitar tradition that King consistently celebrated. Though it is often executed on string 1, string 3 in the root position of the minor pentatonic or blues scale is by far the more common location.

Techniques
Example 6

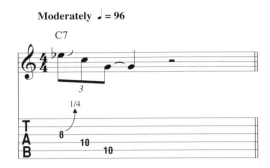

Performance Tip: Pull down on the E♭ with the index finger, followed by the ring and middle fingers for the C and G notes, respectively.

In the figure below, King demonstrates the subtle expressiveness of bending a note one step and releasing it back down before moving forward with the lick. The perception is one of slowing the forward motion dynamically before resuming momentum.

Techniques
Example 7

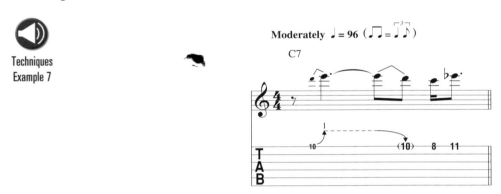

Performance Tip: Bend with the ring finger, backed by the middle and index. Follow with the index (already at fret 8) and then the pinky on fret 11.

Eric Clapton is well-known for his stunning double-string bends, and whether he got the idea from Freddie or one of the other two Kings, for example, is open to conjecture. Nonetheless, Freddie King was apt to employ them judiciously where they would do the most good; for example, over the I chord in measures 1 or 8 in a 12-bar blues progression.

Techniques
Example 8

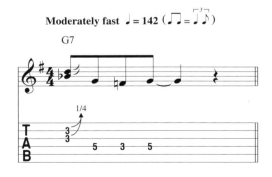

Performance Tip: Pull down with the index finger while maintaining pressure on strings 3–2 with a small barre.

This next example again displays the value of the subtle yet critical quarter-step bend of the ♭3rd to the "true blue note" on string 1 in the "Albert King box" prized by Freddie.

Techniques
Example 9

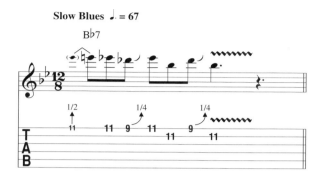

Performance Tip: Bend the E♭ at fret 11 with the ring finger and the D♭ at fret 9 with the index finger. Use the middle finger for the B♭ on string 2 at fret 11 following the E♭. Vibrato the B♭ on beat 3 with the ring finger instead, reinforced with the middle and index.

Blues guitarists often need to resist "letting their fingers do the walking" in the root position of the minor pentatonic or blues scale. The following example contains one lick utilized by King that avoids typical clichés via the reversal of a popular triplet loved by blues cats.

Techniques
Example 10

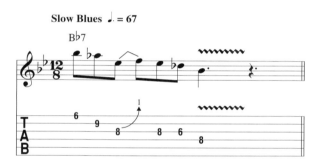

Performance Tip: In sequence, employ the index, pinky, ring (for the bend and the released note), index, and ring finger (for the vibratoed B♭).

STYLISTIC DNA

Phrasing

One of the hidden influences on Freddie King's style was once revealed in a guitar magazine interview in which he cited the fluid alto sax phrasing of '40s jive-talking shuffle king Louis Jordan. Both made the composite blues scale a "major" component in their musical tool box. The figure below contains the ♭3rd bent to the "true blue note" and the major 3rd for the righteous combination of the tangy blues scale and the melodious Mixolydian mode.

DNA
Example 1

Performance Tip: For the ♭3rd at the start and end of the lick, pull downward with the index finger. On beat 2, slide into the major 3rd with the middle finger, followed by the index finger.

The example below is similar, but with the significant addition of the ♭7th (B♭) as the last note in the phrase. As previously "noted," the ♭7th provides anticipation to the next chord change.

DNA
Example 2

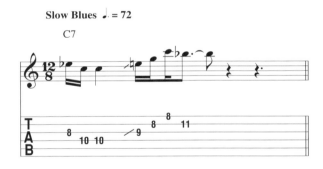

Performance Tip: Use the index and ring fingers to go from the ♭3rd to the root, respectively. End on the ♭7th with the pinky.

Phrasing fluidly does not necessarily mean picking a long line of notes in close intervals. The wide intervals of this next example may also be executed smoothly, particularly in conjunction with the slow bend, which begins and sets the tone of the lick.

DNA
Example 3

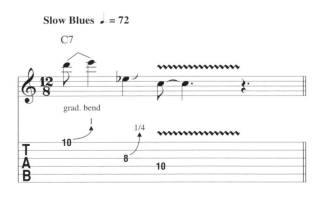

Decades before Eric Clapton was praised by Les Paul for "telling a story" with his expressive licks, Louis Jordan was doing it as a matter of course. Here is a choice example of King "telling a story" in the graceful, horn-like manner of Jordan:

DNA
Example 4

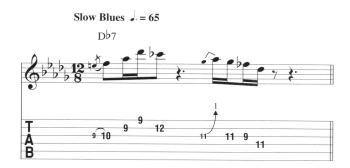

Performance Tip: Barre strings 3–1 at fret 9 with the index finger before hammering from the ♭3rd to the major 3rd and continuing to pick on the way up the scale.

Though Jordan obviously could not bend pitches like a guitarist, his sensually sustained notes show up in King's slinky bends.

DNA
Example 5

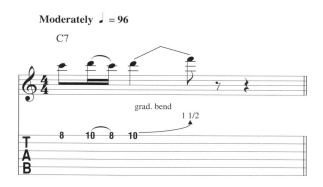

Performance Tip: The index and ring fingers will suffice for the C and the D notes, respectively, with the latter being the one to execute the bend, backed up by the middle and index.

One of the many advantages of the composite blues scale is its virtue of providing melodies via half-step intervals, as seen on beat 1. In addition, this type of phrase contributes fluidity.

DNA
Example 6

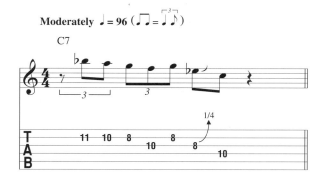

Performance Tip: Use the pinky, ring, and index for the melodic run on string 2. As usual, bend the ♭3rd on string 3 to the "true blue note" by pulling downward with the index finger.

The figure below is a virtual one-measure tutorial on sax-like phrasing in the composite blues scale, with the ♭3rd and major 3rd appearing in order to provide tartness and sweetness, respectively.

DNA

Example 7

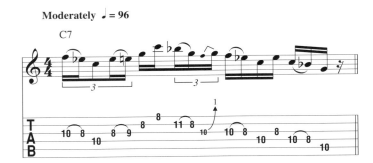

Performance Tip: With the fret hand "finding a home" in eighth position, follow the "one-finger-per-fret" rule, with the index, middle, ring, and pinky fingers accessing frets 8, 9, 10, and 11 on the appropriate strings.

Turnarounds

Turnarounds are traditionally the last two measures in a 12- or 8-bar blues progression. King was an expert at playing personalized single-note turnarounds. The example below contains a basic I–V (G7–D7) riff occurring in measure 12 of a 12-bar blues. Quite simply, the root (G) and 5th (D) notes are emphasized.

DNA

Example 8

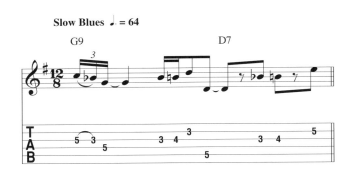

Performance Tip: On beats 2–4, play the ♭3rd with the index finger and the major 3rd with the middle finger.

The turnaround below also consists of the I (C7) and V (G7) chords in measure 12. Observe how the final note is the 5th (D) of G in order to encourage momentum into the next 12-bar verse (not shown).

DNA

Example 9

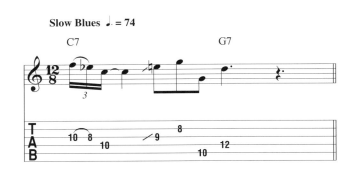

Performance Tip: Slide into the E at fret 9 with the middle finger, followed by the index finger for the G on fret 8.

This next example contains a complete turnaround for measures 11–12 of a 12-bar blues. See how measure 11 (I chord) is as legato and serpentine as any line Louis Jordan ever played. A significant element in King's "DNA" are runs that ascend and descend gracefully while hitting all the essential notes in the composite blues scale with dynamic tension and release.

DNA
Example 10

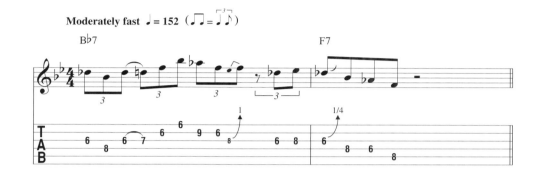

Performance Tip: Execute the one-step bend in measure 11 (the first measure in the example) by pushing upward with the ring finger, backed by the middle finger. Pull downward with the index finger for the quarter-step bend in measure 12.

Turnarounds that signal the *end* of a blues tune resolve to the I chord rather than the V. The example below highlights the value of a repetitive triplet in measure 11 for creating musical tension and even more anticipation to the final resolution—the I (Bb9) chord in measure 12.

DNA
Example 11

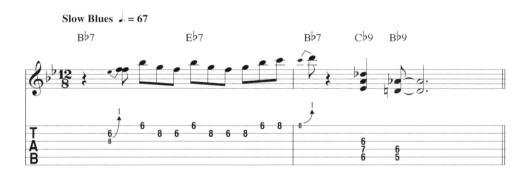

Performance Tip: For the unison bend on beat 1 of measure 11, place the index finger on string 2 at fret 6 and bend string 3 at fret 8 with the ring finger (backed by the middle finger) while striking both strings simultaneously (see photo).

MUST HEAR

Freddie King recorded an immortal and monumental legacy of classic electric blues, both instrumental and vocal. The former, particularly, constitute a "King's ransom" of sensational technique and flat-out musical nourishment. All have been reissued many times, including on CD, and often contain duplication. The original pre-1965 releases will be of the most interest to guitarists. However, all the recordings listed are of value and recommended, especially the compilations with more obscure but worthy early tracks.

Original LP Releases

Freddie King Sings, 1961

Essential Tracks

Have You Ever Loved a Woman
I'm Tore Down
Lonesome Whistle Blues
You've Got to Love Her with a Feeling

Let's Hide Away and Dance Away with Freddy King, 1961

Essential Tracks

Hide Away
Butterscotch
Sen-Sa-Shun
Side Tracked
The Stumble
San-Ho-Zay
Just Pickin'
In the Open

Freddy King Gives You a Bonanza of Instrumentals, 1965

Essential Tracks

The Sad Nite Owl
Remington Ride
Low Tide

Freddie King Is a Blues Master, 1969

Essential Tracks

Play It Cool
Today I Sing the Blues
It's Too Late, She's Gone
Get Out of My Life, Woman

My Feeling for the Blues, 1970

Essential Tracks

Yonder Wall
Ain't Nobody's Business What We Do
The Things I Used to Do
My Feeling for the Blues

Compilations

All His Hits, 1996
(Originally issued in 1965)

Essential Tracks

Christmas Tears
Look Ma, I'm Crying
(The Welfare) Turns Its Back on You
Some Other Day, Some Other Time
Full Time Love

The Best of Freddie King: The Shelter Years, 2000

Essential Tracks

Going Down
Palace of the King
Woman Across the River
Same Old Blues
I'd Rather Be Blind
Reconsider, Baby

Live Albums

Live at the Electric Ballroom, 1974

Essential Tracks

That's Alright (solo acoustic guitar)
Dust My Broom (solo acoustic track)
Key to the Highway
Let the Good Times Roll

Live at the Texas Opry House, 1976
(with Bugs Henderson Band)

Essential Tracks

Your Move
Ain't Gonna Worry Anymore
Boogie on Down

MUST SEE

If you only buy one, it should be *The!!!! Beat*, without question. King is in his prime, before crossing over to the rock audience. Nonetheless, all are invaluable learning and listening experiences.

On DVD

The!!!! Beat, 1966, Vestapol

Live at the Sugarbowl, September 22, 1972, Vestapol

In Concert: Dallas, Texas, January 20, 1973, Vestapol